Harp on the Shore

There was a time when the beauty and the music were all within, and I sat and listened to my thoughts, and there was a song in them...a positive, though faint and distant music, not sung by any bird, nor vibrating any earthly harp...I lay on the rocks, foundered like a harp on the seashore...You sat on the earth as on a raft, listening to music that was not of the earth, but which ruled and arranged it. Man *should be* the harp articulate.

Journal

Willard H. Bonner

Harp on the Shore

Thoreau and the Sea

Edited and Completed by
George R. Levine

State University of New York Press
Albany

for Elda, again

The woodblock illustrations are reproduced from *Select Fables* by Thomas and John Bewick, Newcastle, 1820.

Published by
State University of New York Press, Albany

Printed in the United States of America

For information, address State University of New York Press, State University Plaza, Albany, N.Y., 12246

Library of Congress Cataloging in Publication Data

Bonner, Willard Hallam, 1899-1980
Harp on the shore.

Includes index.
1. Thoreau, Henry David, 1817-1862 — Criticism and interpretation. 2. Sea in literature. 3. Atlantic Ocean in literature. 4. Seashore in literature. 5. Seafaring life in literature. I. Levine, George R. II. Title.
PS3057.S43B6 1985 818′.309 85-2780
ISBN 0-87395-982-5 ISBN 0-87395-981-7 (pbk.)

10 9 8 7 6 5 4 3 2 1

TABLE OF CONTENTS

Preface

When Willard Bonner died in April, 1980, the manuscript of *Harp on the Shore: Thoreau and the Sea* was virtually complete. Although it lacked a final chapter, his intentions for that chapter were quite clear in the notes and preliminary sketches that he left behind. In addition, in 1976 Professor Bonner had published an article on the very subject on which he had decided to conclude his study of Thoreau and the maritime. This article is the basis for Chapter VIII.

In addition to assembling the materials for that final chapter, I have limited my role to that of editor. I have changed only those sections of the manuscript that Professor Bonner himself indicated were in need of revision or which common sense dictated. I have added to the manuscript only on those occasions where I felt there was a need for greater elucidation. In every instance, I have attempted to keep as closely as possible to his ideas and to his habits of phrasing and punctuation. In completing the manuscript, I have benefited from the advice and criticism of my friend and collegue, Professor Robert Daly. The index was prepared by Professor Judith T. Melamed, who was also a friend of Willard Bonner's.

My modest role should not distract attention from the fact that this is Willard Bonner's book. It is the product of a life-long love of the sea—especially of the New England coast—and of the writings of Henry David Thoreau. It is a study that actively occupied his mind and energies for the last twelve years of his life.

I agreed to complete this book not because I could pretend to unusual expertise in Thoreau but simply because Willard Bonner and I had been friends and colleagues for almost two decades. Thoreau knew about such matters when, in *A Week on the Concord and Merrimack Rivers*, he said: "Even the death of friends will inspire us as much as their lives. . . . Their memories will be encrusted over with sublime and pleasing thoughts, as monuments of other men are overgrown with moss; for our friends have no place in the graveyard."

George R. Levine

Buffalo, New York

“The Heroic Age Itself”

It is narrow to be confined to woods and fields and grand aspects of nature only. The greatest and wisest will still be related to men. Why not see men standing in the sun and casting a shadow, even as trees? May not some light be reflected from them as from the stems of trees?

Journal

All that is told of the sea has a fabulous quality to an inhabitant of the land, and all its products have a certain fabulous quality, as if they belonged to another planet.

Cape Cod

I

"The Heroic Age Itself"

CLOSE TO THE HEART of Thoreau's mystery was his vitalism. Live now, he said, live dynamically according to one's lights, in accordance if possible with the laws and rhythms of the universe. Live aggressively according to one's own highest moral and spiritual insights. That he was reticent about sex and held notions about purity too refined for the physical exuberance of our time, do not alter the fact. What he said over and over in phrases familiar to all was: March to whatever music you hear, but march. Sail, but be sure to sail somewhere. Not only be good, be good for something. Dream up castles in Spain, but thereafter put in the foundations. Think with the whole body, "the heart and liver and every member." Live inwardly and strive in the herculean task of thinking a thought and getting it expressed. Look, listen, think—but act.

The unrestrained young commercial nation into which Thoreau was born was nothing if not dynamic and vital, though lacking in some important ingredients. And the resident of a small Massachusetts town like Concord had no way of eluding its influence for better or worse. Thoreau understood his time better than most. The brilliant record of *Walden,* set sharply against the social backdrop, contains most of the familiar barbs he directed against it. His rustication in order to think dazzles us, and we have been overwhelmed by his passion for nature and retirement. Some readers are loath to admit any wholesome reaction to a scene he often paints so darkly. He did, however, respond with continued excitement to one of the age's most spectacular aspects, the maritime scene, which centered chiefly in Boston. He rarely felt free of a conscious presence of the sea with all its bustle and stir, from Long Wharf in Boston to the Fitchburg Railroad cut nearby, from ships engaged in trade with China and the Spice Islands and those probing the death-dealing reaches of the Arctic to his own shoreside confrontations at Plymouth and Cape Cod and Staten Island, Cape Ann and the coast of Maine.

Thoreau read voraciously about the sea—contemporary voyages, sailors' handbooks, even geodetic coast surveys. He strove to understand the sea and its effects on man. He knew about the near slavery of men and boys who sailed before the mast, yet he thought the questing life of a sailor more attractive than that of a farmer. To him the most intrepid men of his time were maritime traders and explorers, especially those who penetrated the Polar seas. This was why he called his century "the heroic age itself." It is a teasing phrase. It is no surprise, therefore, that scenes from and references to the maritime are to be found scattered so widely among his writings.

No one would need reminding that Thoreau's age was the great American age of sail, of which we now are so sentimentally fond: spartangled harbors and long voyages, tall clippers to golden California and the South Seas and China, elaborate scientific expeditions, intrepid and often unscrupulous explorer-traders, California hide and tallow tubs, stubby whalers and sealers, and fast scheduled coastwise and transatlantic packets. This was an age indeed in which the American Navy came into its own and earned its first historian.

What a recent editor of *Walden* has written of that work might be said of the bulk of Thoreau's writings. "His book was steeped in the Concord and New England he loved."[1] The New England that Thoreau loved was a burgeoning, highly homogenous maritime world, the upper end of the Atlantic littoral which was still America's cultural base. Are not America's cities little more than clusters of wharves jutting into harbors, Thoreau mused. The lineaments of this world were common knowledge to all New Englanders, and their common vocabulary was laced with nautical terms. Furthermore, with increase of personal fortunes and with new modes of rapid transportation, non-nautical New Englanders were discovering their own seashore as a place for summer residence or short vacations, where rest, physical and mental therapy, and an extension of esthetic experience might be enjoyed.

Just what was the impact of this world on Concord, Massachusetts, and on the mind and art of Thoreau himself? Thoreau pondered the meaning of the sea, invited it into his consciousness, and symbolized it in his art. He deliberately sought the edge of the sea at Newburyport (Plum Island), Cape Ann, Boston, Cohasset, Plymouth, Cape Cod (especially the Outer Beach), Fair Haven, Fire Island, and Staten Island. He preferred to travel by sloop and packet where possible, rather than by "the cars." He visited the redolent seaports of Portland, Salem, Boston, Plymouth, Wellfleet, Provincetown, New Bedford, and Nantucket. He loitered on the docks of Boston, New Bedford, and that "most completely maritime town" he had ever seen, Provincetown. He recorded data on the natural world where possible, but he also relished gossip with local people, especially old seafaring folk, whose tales he regarded as tinctured with wisdom and myth. The merriest old man he ever knew was an oysterman at Wellfleet, whose oddities he snatched from oblivion in a few paragraphs in *Cape Cod,* the best book on Cape Cod we have.

It was a world of ships. In the great flux of New England commercial life, the principal concern of coastwise men from 1812 on into the 1860's and the 1870's was the building and sailing of wooden ships, and commerce developed from the cargoes they sought and carried. Shipyards all along the coast from the Penobscot and Kennebec rivers to Baltimore and the Virginia Capes launched their thousands to outsail and outtrade the ships of other nations. They covered the globe. Certain American ports and their sea captains acquired fame for carrying on and dominating a single trade; and types of vessels evolved which were most suited to the work or trade at hand. It was common knowledge that in the early decades Salem dominated the pepper and sandalwood trade, her captains (Salem men) characteristically sailing to the Pacific by way of the Cape of Good Hope. Boston on the other hand dominated the Northwest fur trade and the California trade in hides and general merchandise. Her weathered navigators rounded treacherous Cape Horn as part of the season's work.

The great decades of the whalers out of Nantucket and New Bedford were the 40's and 50's. The great decade of the Clippers to California and China out of several New England ports was the 50's. And the harbors of Gloucester, Plymouth, Wellfleet, and Provincetown were like canvas cities when their fishing fleets lay at anchor. Packets raced from Boston and New York to Liverpool; and the great Cunard Line began its regular transatlantic steam passenger service in 1840—to Boston, a great boost to that city's pride. Thoreau's dates we may recall were 1817 to 1863.

Physical evidence of the great maritime urge was always thus near by. But other aspects also contributed to what John A. Christie calls "influence by saturation." Printed accounts of expeditions and other naval adventures flowed from books and journals. New Pacific islands were discovered and reported, and deeper probes were made into both the Arctic and the Antarctic. We have forgotten how many and how strenuous were the explorations into the unknown parts of the world in the nineteenth century.

In general the reason for all this activity was to open up new areas for trade: for whales, seals, tea, spices, sandalwood, *bêche de mere,* furs tortoise and pearl shell. Not only did trade follow exploration, but traders were expected to lose no opportunity to explore and discover. The trader-explorer was a familiar and very acceptable maritime figure. There seemed no end to new discoveries and new riches. Frontier fever was epidemic long before and long after the California gold rush, which itself was interlocked with the racing of clipper ships to the West Coast. It is completely appropriate that the frontispiece in F. O. Matthiessen's brilliant study of "art and expression in the age of Emerson and Whitman" be a portrait, not of a literary man, but of that ex-farm boy Donald McKay, the East Boston builder of the *Flying Cloud* and the *Sovereign of the Seas*. It was completely appropriate also that a trader-explorer figure of considerable dimension appears near the beginning of

Walden, and a lesser one near the end. It was "the type of character," notes Matthiessen, "with which the writers of the age were most concerned, the common man in his heroic stature, or as Whitman called the type, 'Man in the Open Air.'" Cooper and Dana and Melville reflected this vibrant world in their distinguished narratives.

There were also many purely scientific exploring expeditions. Captain James Cook, near though not contemporary, was a hero in Thoreau's mind second only to Columbus. New adventures to the North and South Polar regions were touched off by Cook's descent in the South Pacific to the Antarctic and by his reaching into the North Pacific in search of the Northwest Passage. The account of Cook's last voyage (published in Hartford), which Thoreau read, was written by the irrepressible and famous young American John Ledyard from Groton, Connecticut.

Still fresh in the memory were the voyages of the *Columbia* out of Boston, Captain Robert Gray (of Tiverton, Rhode Island). Gray sailed with Captain John Kendrick of Wareham, Massachusetts, to the Northwest Coast for furs. Gray continued on round the world, the first American to circumnavigate the globe. In a later voyage Gray touched Oregon, claimed it for the United States, and sailed over the bar into the river he named "Columbia" for his ship.

Thoreau's day witnessed and read about classic explorations by such men as Sir James Clark Ross to both the Antarctic and Arctic, Sir William Edward Parry to the Arctic, Charles Wilkes, U.S.N., to the Antarctic, and Sir John Franklin to the Arctic. All these hardy men were scientists as well as navigators and explorers, leaving valuable data in their journals as well as names on the map for stay-at-homes to ponder. Ross and Wilkes respectively led official British and American expeditions. Wilkes, a product of a naval training school in Boston, left a five-volume *Narrative* (published in Philadelphia) that was not only noticed in the transcendentalists' *Dial* but drew Thoreau's fire in *Walden*. It was quite in keeping with the spirit of the times that it was only a political accident that Hawthorne failed to sail on this very expedition and be its historian.[2]

The exploring sensation of the century, however, was occasioned by the voyages of Sir John Franklin "to the shores of the Polar Sea" in search once again of the water passage across the top of the world. Great as these voyages were, they did not by themselves touch the imagination like the thirty-nine separate expeditions sent out in search of Franklin after his disappearance in Lancaster Sound on his third voyage. These search-and-relief expeditions, both public and private, British and American, have "no parallel in maritime annals," wrote J.K. Laughton. While carrying on the ten-year search, they also "turned the map of the Arctic regions of North America from a blank void into a grim but distinct representation of islands, straits, and seas." Thoreau shows that he was impressed. The most distinguished encourager and supporter of these ventures was the American shipping magnate, Henry Grinnell, who grew up in the whaling town of New Bedford and was never thereafter deaf to the call of the sea. Expeditions in 1850 and 1853 were financed by him, the first wholly and the second in large part. They were well known as the First and Second Grinnell Expeditions, though Grinnell did not command them. A Philadelphian, Dr. Elisha Kane, sailed as surgeon on the First, organized and commanded the Second, and was the historian of both. His *Arctic Explorations* (2 vols., Phila., 1856) was the kind of book that made a fortune for his publishers and, so it is said, "lay for a decade with the Bible on almost literally every parlor table in America."

As we look back now it is astonishing to see how many Polar probes there were. Thus polar ice as well as fair South Sea isles often figure in Thoreau's imagery. He knew so much about exploration that when Emerson recommended that Thoreau take over an issue of the *Dial* in Emerson's absence, he quite naturally (and humorously) described "this young man" as competent to be "leader of any Pacific exploration." Floundering through a swamp one January day Thoreau quietly remarked, "This is instead of a Polar Sea expedition and going after Franklin."[3]

Very early the scientific and cultural importance of New England maritime trade was felt. Of special interest among the various historical and scientific groups that evolved in Boston and Salem was the Salem East India Marine Society. Ernest S. Dodge, curator of the Peabody Museum, tells us that the Salem society was founded as early as 1799 "to collect natural and artificial curiosities to be found beyond Cape Horn and the Cape of Good Hope" and that a member had to be a Salem captain who had rounded one of the two capes. The Society required the captains to keep journals, deposit them with the Society, and bring back material.[4] Thoreau visited the "East India Marine Hall" at least once. In a few years the collections were large enough to warrant the pubication of catalogs in 1821 and 1831. When the Peabody Museum took the Society over in the 1860's, there were over 400 members. One wonders how many were still Salem captains.

Whoever takes the final measure of Thoreau must give some attention to the influence of this brilliant and colorful period, remembering all the time that men and ships like these were visible in any port Thoreau visited. They were elements of life, not, as to us, nostalgic recollections. Yet except for discussions of some of Thoreau's metaphors which only incidentally happen to be nautical, and for stimulating comments in John A. Christie's *Thoreau-World Traveler* (1965), such matters have so far drawn little significant critical comment. However, several of Thoreau's basic concepts are repeatedly vivified by maritime and nautical images, and for a lack of understanding of this aspect of his world and of his taste for it, certain meanings appearing in his writings can be lost or left annoyingly vague.

We are all familiar, for example, with Thoreau's ecstasies in the *Journal* and in the Monday section of *A Week on the Concord and Merrimack Rivers* over the telegraph, when wires for that new electric marvel were strung along the Fitchburg railroad and began to hum and to make the poles and even the adjacent fence posts hum. But what does Thoreau mean in *Walden* when he begins to describe his "business" at the Pond, attending to sunrises and listening (*outside* the town) to "what was in the wind," carrying it "express," or telegraphing "any new arrival" from the top of some cliff or tree? Common nautical practice tells us. His metaphor embodies the famous semaphore system, common to all the navies and commercial ships of the world, by which vessels spoke to one another, and by which in New England names and news of ships passing Nantucket and Cape Cod were flashed by relays in a matter of minutes to Central Wharf, Boston, and to ship owners there awaiting the arrival sometimes days later, of their ships. Thoreau had visited "telegraph stations" on Staten Island and Cape Cod, and briefly describes one at Hull, Massachusetts.[5]

Understanding Thoreau's application of some quite familiar nautical phrases also helps us to know his critical position with regard to winter. Opposing views (and apparently conflicting statements by Thoreau himself) have left us unclear. Did winter exhilarate or depress him? Early sentimental editor-critics have over-stressed his rugged relish of winter landscape. On the other hand, an inevitable critical backlash today plays up his feelings in the early fifties of depression at the onset of winter as touchstones of his despair and a paralyzing sense of failure. Nautical metaphors, however, like "bound out" and "getting in" shift the balance and direct us (as we shall see later) to a figure of paramount importance, the idea of mental and of sense experience as adding up to a complete round trip voyage, two complementary parts of the whole.

The very onwardness of life implicit in his metaphor of the voyage, or a series of voyages, extends our too narrowly confined notion of Thoreau merely as a retirement-loving man of the fields and woods and streams. He seems to have had an ever-present feeling of fluid motion, undulation, a reaching out and a flowing toward new, or at least renewable, life. However quiet he was, celebrating a stillness that merges with divine illumination, he saw himself as a traveler. His body may have been static, his mind never. The same sanity that he insisted came from getting *into* the world of nature was achieved on many occasions by getting *out* into the busy world he is so often thought to have spurned. Hence his *exit from* Walden, setting a new course, having as he said several more lives to live, with no time now for the old one. This vital continuum is set forth in one of his most famous maritime figures.

Part of the present study will be historical, based on the sound assumption that thorough understanding of social and historical contexts will aid us in literary comprehension. The *how* and the *why* do aid in the *what,* to borrow and slightly distort Matthiessen's terms regarding possible approaches to the works of the five great American authors. Or as Leo Marx puts it with regard to American fables, "It is necessary to understand the interplay between the literary imagination and what happens outside literature."

The maritime world rendered Thoreau enormous enrichment in mind and art, extending beyond vivid rhetorical devices to such philosophical concepts as 1) his notion of man's struggle to attain individuality and identity, 2) his notion of Homeric or Edenic man, and 3) his notion that some middle ground was best where man can and should stand, between such things as the natural and the civilized, the commercial and the free spirit, the active and the static, the individual and the group, the finite and the infinite. Most important in the last named was his symbolism of the seashore where man always must ultimately stand and where he can be as responsive to divine winds as an aeolian harp.

Literal and symbolic nautical language burdens this study often because it is present in Thoreau in some bulk. Indeed I was first lured into a second and third look because of it. His command of it was lifelong, although it became more seasoned and significant through long use and his own increasing contact with the sea.

The materials presented here support some views already held about Thoreau, but they should also shift some hitherto misdirected emphases. Most of all it is hoped they will aid in the imaginative reading of a man who first and last, as he himself declared, thought and wrote poetically. Pursuing these matters has shown me that the neurotic, death-haunted Thoreau that Perry Miller argued for in *Consciousness in Concord* must be offset by a Thoreau well endowed with sanity and well-honed good sense and a profound commitment to persistent clear-eyed inquiry. A similar adjustment is called for with regard to the arguments of other restless recent writers like Leo Stoller who, annoyed by a century of impulsive adulation, see Thoreau as a mystical idealist collapsing after the "failure" of the Walden experiment and capitulating to the westward-coursing world of wealth and power. Thoreau's feeling for the one great vehicle of the Westward movement, the ships and men that made the link between the old world and the new, however, shows something different. He was energized by the reality and stirred by recognition of its symbolic meaning. His reaction was like that which caused him to pause during one of his rural walks in 1853 and to search for the poetry in the simple practical acts of men repairing a stone bridge, telling himself; "You may be excused if you are always pathetic, but do not refuse to recognize." In his effort to recognize the position of Americans in both nature and human society, he is closer to John Locke's symbol of Eden as an America than he is to the Berkeleyan cliché about the westward course of empire. Thoreau's unquenchable vitalism was stimulated ever anew by the heroic qualities of contemporary seafaring men, whose acts stirred his faith in the possibilities of achieving and expressing inner qualities of life possible in an ever new world. He modified Locke by extending the meaning of *west*, and unhestitatingly recognizing the shores of America as symbolic Eden fit for hardy new arrivals from the sea.

The New England maritime world thus functioned as a catalyst in Thoreau's thinking about himself, his era, and the history of Western man. He came to realize that consciousness is bound by what exists, and the objective world is bound by what it has become, as Gertrude Lenzer recently remarked in another connection.[6] He also knew there are infinite and unrealized aspects of the human psyche to be touched, if ever, by individual insight. He knew that in the process of comprehending the world, his mind also had to comprehend what that world was not and what potentially it might be. Paraphrasing Professor Lenzer further, because her remark fits Thoreau so well, "is" and "ought" are inseparable, but the "ought" can only be realized in action. That action impelled Thoreau to insist poetically that his whole life was a long ocean voyage of discovery, that man was always a dweller by a vast and little known sea, and that the New World was but the new home of wrecked mariners—an extended Robinson Crusoe myth.

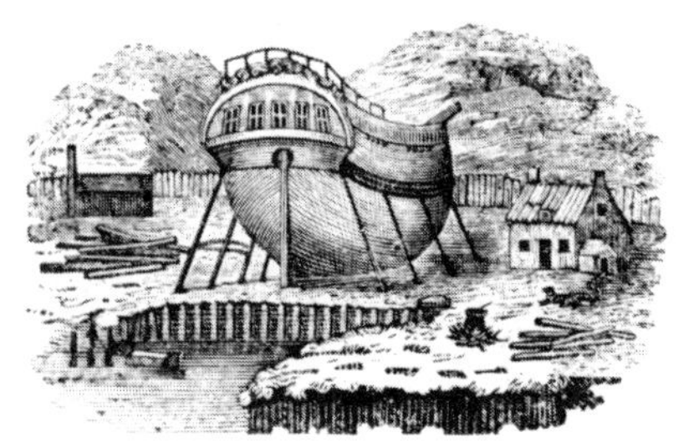

Thoreau's Native Port

Our town, after all, lies but farther up a creek of the universal sea.

Journal

You may go round the world before the mast, but not behind the plow.

Journal

II

Thoreau's Native Port

THE LITTLE WORLD OF CONCORD always lay close to the sea, participating willy nilly in New England's lively maritime life. Thoreau by no means strains at metaphor when in *Life Without Principle* he speaks of himself as a Concord sailor boy, "sauntering in [his] native port," pondering the advertisements for able-bodied seamen and embarking on his "voyage" as soon as he was of age.

In the first half of the nineteenth century Concord was hardly an inland town, although the original settlers two centuries removed had deliberately moved away from the seaboard and taken up frontier land specifically in order to farm, to subsist from the soil peacefully in a community they had asked to be allowed to call "Concord." But as things turned out, seventeen miles was not far enough. By Thoreau's time the world they had abandoned had stretched and swelled until Concord had been absorbed, as it is today, to a degree by Boston. Thoreau knew very well that he was bound to the Atlantic littoral when he protested, "Let us be a town and not a suburb."[1]

But Boston reached out, her commerce flowing in and out to all parts and ports of the world. Anyone within her zone of influence daily absorbed a world of knowledge and information about the sea and shipping. Even the railroad when it came, taking over from the canal and turnpike, at first only bound Concord the closer to the Hub. The axle on which the Hub turned was Long Wharf, an institution of strong significance to Thoreau. He points with interest and perhaps pride several times to the fact that his grandfather had a place of business on it. Long Wharf, he said, was the first place in Boston he visited whenever he went to the city; and the end of the narrative in his *Cape Cod* presents a lively picture of the Wharf's thronging life, including the execution in the gathering dusk of a perfect running moor by the skipper of the yacht *Olata*.

For this and other reasons the sea was never long out of Thoreau's consciousness. He often reminded himself that Concord lay only just above the head of tidewater. The break-up of the ice in the spring carried its own sharp reminder, the appearance of seagulls. "They came annually a-fishing like royal hunters to remind us of the sea and that our town, after all, lies but farther up a creek of the universal sea, above the head of tide." They completed the Concord scene, he said, "beating like a vessel in the air." In windy March "it is akin to seeing a mackerel schooner on the coast. It is the nearest approach to sailing vessels in our scenery. . . . Oh, how it salts our fresh, our sweet watered Fair Haven all at once to see this sharp-beaked, greedy sea-bird. . . . We are so far maritime, do not dwell beyond the range of the seagoing gull, the littoral birds. . . . He is never to me perfectly in harmony with the scenery, but like the high water, something unusual."[2]

The peetweet had the same effect on him. Ornithologists today take pains to tell us that in New England the otherwise ubiquitous spotted sandpiper (the peetweet) nests *along the seashore*. "The peetweet," our only beach-bird, teetering along the shore of the Concord river at the Falls near Billerica, reminded Thoreau that this was "an arm of the ocean stream." Migrating geese were messengers of the season's change, "those annual steamers of the air," and the residents of Concord, like those at Hudson's Bay, might "expect the annual vessel which brings the spring."[3]

Up the creeks of "the universal sea" also came the shad, the salmon, and the alewives. Before the mill dams went in, they had streamed in surging masses annually up the Merrimac and the Concord rivers. A Captain Thomas Whitman of nearby Stow in 1880 recalled having seen 1100 shad and eight or ten thousand alewives taken in a single haul—a profitable haul indeed, as shad were worth five dollars a hundred pounds, salmon ten cents a pound.[4] Thoreau twice picturesquely protested the choking off of this living flow from the sea. The inventory of fish in the Saturday section of the *Week* ends in a two fold celebration of the shad. The first is a backward look, reminding the reader that Concord men were once commercial fishermen ("whose seines lie rotting in the garrets of their children"), and that the famous Concord train-band acquired the nickname "The Shad" in those plentiful days because their Captain, having gone fishing on the May day set for spring drill, never showed up. The second is a forward look, an apostrophe to the Shad urging him to keep "a stiff fin" and patiently await the distant day when the Corporation and its Billerica dam would be no more and the river would be opened up once again to visitants from the sea. Thoreau was to repeat the scene and theme, with additions, a decade later when he visited New Bedford.

The runs of anadromous fish were important to Thoreau because fishing for them provided a valuable quality of life in village communities, and becaue the fish symbolized a current of the human spirit that man cannot afford to lose. He urged his New Bedford friend Daniel Ricketson to make his *History of New Bedford* (then in process) a "local and villageous book" full of sketches. Ricketson disregarded this advice, and it was left to Thoreau to present local and villageous scenes. On April 9, 1857, Thoreau went "to the cove south of the town" to "see them haul" alewives. Two days later he went to the head of the Acushnet River "to see them catch smelts." "The shore half a dozen rods on either side was lined with fishers, each wielding a single net." The smelt had been running a month, the herring a fortnight, but the shad had not begun. "Bass, sea perch, pickerel, eels, and sometimes a trout" were also lifted out. "A good part of the village appeared to be collected on the bridge.... The villagers were talking across the stream, calling to each other in their Christian names. Even mothers mingled with the fishermen, looking for their children. It suggested how much we had lost out of Concord River without realizing it. This is the critical season of a river, when it is fullest of life, its flowering season.... If salmon, shad, and alewives were pressing up our river now, as formerly they were, a good part of the villagers would thus, no doubt, be drawn to the brink at this season.... The very fishes...are driven out of a river by the *improvements* of civilized man.... I can hardly imagine a greater change than this produced by the influence of man in nature.... In what sense now does spring ever come to the river.... It is as if some vital quality were to be lost out of man's blood." A vitality from the sea.

Other natural phenomena reminded Thoreau of the sea. There was the "sea-turn." This phrase, still in common use in eastern Massachusetts and other parts of New England, was a very satisfactory description of abrupt changes in temperature occurring usually in the warm seasons when an east wind brings chilling air, along with fog from the Atlantic. It can be fairly sudden and generally comes as a relief. This phenomenon fascinated Thoreau and figures prominently in his well-known interest in aerial phenomena. This cold on-shore wind was as direct a connection with the sea as the sound of breakers would have been. One September, when such a fog bank drifted in, his aunt "thought she could smell the salt marsh in it."[5]

The Concord, the Merrimac, and other local rivers were never merely rivers to Thoreau. Aside from the imaginative extension of them in the *Week*, he saw them as vital connectors with the sea. This was always a vivid fact. Falling on the ice one winter day, he spilled a bucket of sap and immediately thought not of his loss, but of how the sap would ere long "sweeten the sea." When the powder mills blew up, he watched the mile-wide cloud drift east carrying the news "seaward," and later let his imagination follow the debris to sea and beyond. Some blackened timbers, he said, "were carried down to the Merrimack, and by the

Merrimack to the ocean, till perchance they got into the Gulf Stream and were cast up on the coast of Norway, covered with barnacles, or who can tell what more distant strand?. . .

"Mingling with the wrecks of vessels, which communicate a different tale, this wreck of a powder-mill was cast up on some outlandish strand, and went to swell the tide of driftwood collected by some native. Shouldered by whales. Alighted on at first by the muskrat and the peetweet,—and finally perhaps by the stormy petrel and the beach-birds. It is long before Nature forgets it."[6] The mill debris became a link with universal experience.

This keen awareness accounts for the description of Plum Island (at the mouth of the Merrimac) in the *Week* and his exuberance over canal boats and boatmen. Sometimes he stubbornly pursues the point. He presses rather far his identification of "River-weed" growing on a rock in the rapid water of the falls of the Concord, lightly setting aside the identification by Gray and by Torrey, reigning botanists, and insisting on its saltwater kinship. To him it was marine rockweed. "It seemed as if our river had there for a moment anticipated the sea, suffered a sea-change, mimicked the great ocean stream. . . . It is a foretaste of the sea."[7]

Daily reminders of the sea washed into Concord in common gossip and in the newspapers, or were blown in by great storms. "It has rained all day," Thoreau noted in October of 1853, "filling the streams. Just after dark high southerly winds arise, but very warm, blowing rain against the windows and roof and shaking the house. It is very dark withal so that I can hardly find my way to a neighbor's. We think of vessels on the coast, and shipwrecks, and how this will bring down the remaining leaves. . . ." The fall hurricanes drove inland then, as they do now, carrying occasional exhausted pelagic birds like the stormy petrel and the dovekie or the little auk. An unmistakable implication in the opening of *Cape Cod* reveals that at times the hurricanes brought the very salt of the ocean to Concord. Speaking of his inveterate absorption with the Concord landscape, he warns the reader that "having come so fresh to the sea, I have got but little salted. My readers must expect only so much saltness as the land breeze acquires from blowing over an arm of the sea, or is tasted on the windows and the bark of trees twenty miles inland, after September gales." As his point here is the saltness of Cape Cod *vis-á-vis* Concord, the "twenty miles inland" fixes the reader's mind on Concord and gives us an amusing picture of Thoreau going about his house after a severe storm tasting the salt that had clouded the window panes and dried on the windward side of trees.

All accounts of violent storms reported in Concord's *Yeoman's Gazette* and its successors, furthermore, are of damage done to ships, shipping, wharves, and other installations that serve shipping—accounts reprinted from New York, Boston, and other seaboard newspapers. Any reporting of purely local damage is noticeable by its absence. Such an account of the great storm of April 27-28, 1835 in the Concord *Freeman*, for example, runs to an almost unprecendented column and is entirely concerned with ships and docks. A number of notations in his *Journal* indicate that Thoreau regularly was affected by these accounts. "I expect to hear of shipwrecks and of damage done by the tide," he wrote almost in the midst of "a violent northeast storm" on April 19, 1852. And speaking (with a conspicuous nautical phrase) of the great wild birds to be seen "in great storms like this, " he remarks, "When the storm increases, then these great birds that carry the mail of the seasons lay to." You may catch butterflies in pleasant sunny weather, but if you want to see the wildest fowl, go forth "when the storm rages that lays prostrate the forest and wrecks the mariner."[8]

When he reviewed J. A. Etzler's *Paradise Within the Reach of All Men* and treated the subject of power from the winds and waves, Thoreau assumed what every one knew: "Every gazette brings accounts of the untutored freaks of the wind,—shipwrecks and hurricanes which the mariner and planter accept as special or general providences. . . ." Once when examining a great white oak blown down by yet another April storm, he identified the storm as the same one "which destroyed the lighthouse." What lighthouse it was, he felt no need to record. (It was the lighthouse on Minott's Ledge, swept away in April 1851.) Thoreau scanned the papers for the first news of the breaking up of the ice in the Penobscot River in Maine, the conditions of Boston Harbor, or the return of fishing vessels. He responded to the excitement and danger of the life of the Banks fisherman. A single sentence at the end of the *Journal* entry for October 22, 1855 has a certain lonely eloquence: "The Plymouth fishermen have just come home from the Banks, except one."[9]

Thoreau encountered seafaring people in and around Concord. Many old families in the small town had in their history not very far back fishermen, sailors, sea captains, or U.S. Naval personnel. Thoreau provides an amusing anecdote in *Cape Cod* about a boyhood friend. "One of my playmates, who was apprenticed to a printer, and was somewhat of a wag, asked his master one afternoon if he might go a-fishing, and his master consented. He was gone three months. When he came back, he said he had been to the Grand Banks, and went to setting type again as if only an afternoon had intervened." So close to the village print shop were the Grand Banks. "It is remarkable," he wrote, "that, of the four fishermen who most frequent this river,—Melvin, Goodwin and the two Haynses,—the last three have all been fishermen of the sea, have visited the Grand Banks, and are well acquainted with Cape Cod." Shoreside mariners Thoreau seems to accept as a natural part of the landscape. Up the Merrimac, at a lock-man's house "there sits the brother who follows the sea, their representative man; who knows only how far it is to the nearest port, no more distances, all the rest is sea and distant capes,—patting the dog, or dandling the kitten in arms that were stretched by the cable and the oar, pulling against Boreas or the trade-winds. He looks up at the stranger, half pleased, half astonished, with a mariner's eye, as if he were a dolphin within a cast." In that odd excrescent Chapter III in Sanborn's *Henry D. Thoreau* we find further evidence of people who linked Concord with the sea. Duncan Ingraham, a profane, flamboyant sea captain retired from the Surinam trade, was Concord's richest citizen, his house the largest, his church pew the most lavishly upholstered and adorned. His memory was still green in Concord in Thoreau's time, drawing from the surveyor-philosopher a dry comment in his *Journal* about such kinds of old "respectability." Duncan's son was a bold and adventurous American naval officer; and one Joseph Perry went to sea with Paul Jones.[10] When Thoreau went aboard the packet, *Washington Irving*, to see Emerson off to Europe, he was pleased that up to that time the first mate had been "one Stephens, a Concord boy."

There was plenty of folklore of the sea. "My mother says that, visiting once at Captain Pulsifer's at the North End, two sea-captains' wives told the girl, when the things were carried out to be replenished, not to turn out their slops, as it would drown their husbands who were at sea."[11] Thoreau was surprised that Minott, that most poetical of farmers, who had read the *Naval Monument* through, had seen the seashore only once. On the purely oral side there were sea chanteys and buried treasure legends. "Tom Bowline" was Thoreau's favorite song. He also sang "The Bay of Biscay" and the ballad of "Captain Kidd," which were also popular in the parlors of the age. Concord, along with a thousand other places from South Carolina to Nova Scotia, had its buried treasure legends. "Captain Kidd" was still a witching name and drew after it loosely related phrases like "Kidd's men" and "in the days of Captain Kidd." This contact with the Atlantic pirates of a century before was brought about by a resurgence in the 1840's of a money-digging fever traceable to the known practices of pirates like Kidd who returned to American shores and dispersed their booty-laden crews up the estuaries and rivers from Accomack in Virginia to Delaware Bay and points north. These colorful adventurers were universally known as "Kidd's men" no matter with whom they sailed. The most famous Massachusetts legend centered in Palmer and Warren near Springfield. But Concord had its own, which Thoreau ran onto one day in 1854 when in his boat he passed by John Hosmer's Hollow.[12] Hosmer and Anthony Wright hailed him and proceeded to tell him the story of a 6 × 6 × 6 foot hole that money-diggers had recently made. It is a conventional "Kidd" legend (deriving from Poe's *Gold Bug* and from the actual Gardiner's Island adventures of the returned Kidd). Three pirates with their boots and hats stuffed with coins demand a cache in "old Mr. Wood's" cellar, and being refused through fear, ask for earthen pots and a lanthorn. They go out into the Hollow to bury their treasure, followed at a discreet distance by an unnamed townswoman. John Hosmer rather believed the tale, as his father's plow had once turned up three antique bottles, and old Moll Pitcher, who was consulted, advised digging along a line from an apple tree to the place of the bottles. A number of people at various times had dug at this spot. Thus did the East India pirate "trade" and Capt. Kidd touch Concord. And thus it is of Capt. Kidd that Thoreau thinks as he returns from the village to Walden Pond on a dark night, quoting (and doubtless singing) "My name was Captain Kidd, as I sailed." It is one of the gayer moments in *Walden.* Twice later Thoreau speaks of his pleasure in thinking of the money-diggers' hole and his own profit in reaping the only fruit ever produced from that loosened soil—early blackberries. Also in *Walden*[13] he retells another local tale derived from typical pirate lore, of a sunken chest that periodically floated ashore only to disappear back into the depths when anyone approached it.

With the sole exception of the anecdotes about his picturesque bachelor uncle Charles, the most spirited notes in Thoreau's *Journal* about his relatives are those about his sea-going forebearers. With obvious relish he related stories of his cousin Nahum Jones and his paternal grandfather, Jersey Islander Jean Thoreau. On his mother's side were sailors, sea captains, and sail makers. The story of Nahum Jones' cat, derived from Thoreau's Aunt Louisa's recollection of a visit to the Down East Joneses, suggests that many such anecdotes probably passed back and forth in the Thoreau household. Aunt Louisa's "cousin Nahum Jones. . .carried a cat to the West Indies, sold his vessel there; and though the same vessel did not return, and he came back in another vessel without the cat, the cat got home to Gouldsboro [Maine] somehow, unaccountably, about the same time that he did. Capt. Woodward told her that he carried the same cat three times around the world."[14]

Jean Thoreau, Thoreau's grandfather, though he moved to Concord in 1800 and lived there during the last year of his life, was nevertheless a Boston man, a "merchant" on Long Wharf and nearby State Street. When the Revolution came and he was thrown out of work (he was a sail maker and cooper), he returned to privateering. He probably served on the *General Lincoln*, Captain Barnes, and may have served in some sort of engagement with Paul Revere.[15] After such a nautical career, he set up in business on Boston's famous Long Wharf, serving all comers from goods unloaded from ships before his very door, starting with a single "hogshead of sugar" and ending well off by the standards of the day, with several pieces of property in Boston and cash and other tokens of wealth, the whole running to the value of $25,000. An adventurous and a successful life for a man who lived to be only forty-seven.

Conversations about Jean Thoreau in the Thoreau household were relaxed and of considerable interest, if we may build on the entries in the *Journal* in 1853, 1855, and 1856, wherein Thoreau reports the stories told by his sister Helen and his father. Modern biographers have added a few corroborating details.[16] Thoreau thus inherited a close connection with seafaring life and showed interest in the fact.

Not to be overlooked in the last communications between the Thoreaus of the Island of Jersey and the Thoreaus of America is the quaint personal touch to be seen in the manner of sending letters from Europe to America in the first years of the century. Peter Thoreau sent letters by way of his old friend Captain John Harvey of Boston, or by way of one Captain Tousel, whose vessel along with several from Jersey, made annual voyages to Boston. One of the commonest acts of social communication, the sending of a letter, therefore, was never far separated from the ships and captains who conveyed it. Aunt Maria placed such letters in Thoreau's hands for safe keeping. One surmises that this has something to do with Thoreau's seagulls in a storm—ships carrying mail.

To return to Long Wharf and its subtle, irresistible influence on life in Concord and on the imagination of Thoreau. Thoreau's grandfather had some sort of retail business establishment at numbers 43 and 45, Long Wharf. We know that he was in partnership at one time with a man named Hayse and at another with a man named Phillips. He seems to have started alone with the famous barrel of sugar. Peter Thoreau (of Jersey) has heard of the firm of "Thoreau and Hayse"; and Captain Snow of Cohasset told Henry Thoreau that he remembered "hearing fishermen say they fitted out at Thoreau's." The Boston *Directory* for 1796 lists Thoreau as "grocer, No. 43 Long Wharf, house Bridge's Lane;" but Captain Snow's recollection (especially the phrase "fitted out") would suggest that the "store" dealt also in ships' stores and possibly gear. Jean Thoreau, therefore, may have been a kind of ship chandler as well as a "merchant." The latter was the covering term among many used in the old directories to describe a man who had a wharf business establishment.[17]

What can easily escape us here is the picture of Long Wharf and its importance to Henry David Thoreau when he went there "first" and gazed at what was certainly one of the century's most romantic and fascinating scenes—waterfront activity in the heyday of the clippers, packets, and coasters. In attempting to recapture some of this, one may take his cue from Thoreau himself, who saw quite clearly that the wharves symbolized Boston, and that Long Wharf was the representative wharf.

Internationally famous for its length and accommodations, it surged with men and goods, "a general resort of all the inhabitants and... more frequented, we think, than any other part of town," wrote Thomas Pemberton.[18] Boston's harbor, with 17 feet of water at low tide could accommodate, as the Boston *Directory* for 1795 boasted, 500 vessels at anchor at the same time. As Samuel Eliot Morison tells us, in 1845 "the most prosperous decade in the maritime history of Massachusetts was just beginning." The 3,000 foreign and 6,000 coast-wise entries into Boston Harbor during this period made it apparent that Boston was rapidly catching up on New York.[19]

From his Harvard days on, Thoreau responded as enthusiastically to the vitality of commerce as he did abhorrently to its venality. At Harvard he associated it with the freedom of the new world. In the "Sounds" section of *Walden* he thrilled to its "enterprise and bravery." It was "unexpectedly confident and serene, alert, adventurous, and unwearied." It was all this that drew him to Long Wharf, where he went "naturally straight through the city to the end." "What are our maritime cities but shops and dwellings of merchants, about a wharf projecting into the sea, where there is a convenient harbor." On May 9, 1854 he wrote, "Sat on end of Long Wharf. Was surprised to observe that so many of the men on board the shipping were pure countrymen in dress and habits, and the seaport is no more than a country town to which they come a-trading.... As I watched the various craft unfurling their sails and getting to sea, I felt more than for years inclined to let the winds blow me also to other climes."

The passage is of interest for the double nature of his response: nostalgic yearning to go to sea and awareness of the indigenous rusticity of the scene. When he later reworked the material in *Cape Cod*, the romantic posture disappeared, and the scene seemed simply to be like that at any country fair. Here surprise gives way to satisfaction in the fact that the shore end of the shipping business was conducted after all by his own shirtsleeved countrymen "from Maine and Pennsylvania" steering their teams about among the goods and clutter.[20] His final sense of the moment seems to have been the inter-relation or point of contact of maritime and rural scene, taking Concord with him, as Emerson said, always.

Concord newspapers in the late thirties and the forties not only gave generous space to shipping news, but editorialized for the descendents of the first Concordians (who had moved west in order to escape the city) on the virtues and good influence of "Boston and Her Steam Navigation." Every farmer, said the *Yeoman's Gazette* as early as May 4, 1839, will be the better for it. The Cunard Line, about which this editorial was written, was almost a public institution. Ship arrivals were reported, and record trans-Atlantic runs were boasted of. Boston Harbor, however, had a bad habit of freezing over in midwinter in Thoreau's century. It did so seven times within the span of his memory. One of these impediments to commercial fortune sealed up the Harbor in late January and early February of 1844 after the arrival of Cunard's sidewheeler the *Britannia*, one of the first Atlantic liners to operate out of Boston on a fixed schedule. To Boston merchants it was unthinkable that the ship be held up and the reputation of Boston, in her competition with New York, be damaged. Accordingly they rallied to the crisis and assembled a vast army of professional ice cutters (men, horses, and saws) to cut and keep open a 14-17 mile ship channel. This had to be done several seasons. On January 24, 1858, having read about such a freeze-up, Thoreau went to see it, though the temperature was fourteen degrees below zero. "A.M. at Cambridge and Boston," he wrote in his *Journal*. "Saw Boston Harbor frozen over.... Reminded me of, I think, Parry's Winter Harbor, with vessels frozen. Saw thousands on the ice, a stream of men reaching down to Fort Independence, where they were cutting a channel toward the city. Ice said to reach fourteen miles. Snow untracked on many decks."

There were other ways in which Concord was pulled toward Boston and her impatient ships. Because of Thoreau's *Walden*, the affair of Walden Pond's ice and the great ice trade of Frederic Tudor is famous. The persevering and ruthless Tudor, who had established himself as king of the ice trade, reached out for Walden's ice when his commercial superiority was threatened, and when sources of ice nearer Boston had been exhausted or preempted. The passage in *Walden* tells how "a hundred men of Hyperborean extraction" swooped down on the pond with carloads of strange tools. Every day they "came from Cambridge to get out 10,000 tons of ice." It was piled up in a giant obelisk thirty-five feet high and six or seven rods square. It was never shipped, but endured under its cover of hay and boards for a year and a half. The "Winter" section ends with philosophical musings that would not be there but for Tudor, the ice king, who made fame and fortune by introducing ice into tropical countries in insulated double-hulled ships. In the morning, writes Thoreau, he read the *Bhagvat-Geeta*. "I lay down the book and go to my well for water, and lo! there I meet the servant of the Bramin, priest of Brahma and Vishnu and Indra...come to draw water for his master, and our buckets as it were grate together in the same well. The pure Walden water is mingled with the sacred water of the Ganges. With favoring winds it is wafted past the site of the fabulous islands of Atlantis and Hesperides...melts in the tropic gales of the Indian seas, and is landed in ports of which Alexander only heard the names." There is almost as much of Frederic Tudor as of Thoreau here.

Long Wharf was more than a country fair and a landing stage for ships. It was the center of radiating channels of commerce that carried forth the cargoes of newly arrived ships and brought back construction materials and cargoes to fill up the ships again. Once again *Walden* and the *Journal* give us the picture in the landings of the Fitchburg railroad. It was a transportation pattern established long before the railroads by the canals. Concord received and shipped goods by boat. The termini of the railroads were the wharves. The terminus of the ill-fated Middlesex Canal was the tide water of the Charles River basin. There is therefore almost as much fact as fancy when Thoreau in two major works calls Concord a port. It was.

The vivid description in *Walden* of the Fitchburg Railroad, as its train roars by the track-walking Thoreau, is in the section called "Sounds." It is, however, more full of sights and smells than sounds. "I smell the stores which go dispensing their odors all the way from Long Wharf to Lake Champlain, reminding me of foreign parts, of coral reefs, and Indian oceans, and tropical climes, and the extent of the globe. I feel more like a citizen of the world at the sight of the palm-leaf. . . the Manilla hemp and cocoanut husks, the old junk, gunny bags. . . . This carload of torn sails is more legible and interesting now than (if they should be) wrought into paper and printed books. . . . Here goes lumber from the Maine woods, which did not go out to sea in the last freshet. . . Thomaston lime. . . rags in bales. . . . This closed car smells of salt fish, the strong New England and commercial scent, reminding me of the Grand Banks and the fisheries. . . . Next Spanish hides. . . . Here is a hogshead of molasses. . . directed to John Smith of Cuttingsville, Vermont [and]. . . advertised in the Cuttingsville Times." These redolent things go up. Cattle, and pine for masts, go down.

Before the railroad, the old Middlesex Canal had played precisely this part, linking in Thoreau's boyhood the two Concords (New Hampshire and Massachusetts) with the sea. In the Tuesday section of the *Week* Thoreau describes at some length the canal boats and the boatmen of the Merrimac. "They commonly carry down wood or bricks,—fifteen or sixteen cords of wood, and as many thousand bricks at a time,—and bring back stores for the country, consuming two or three days each way between Concord, New Hampshire, and Charlestown." The Canal crossed the Concord River at Billerica not far from Concord, Massachusetts, which town was linked into the system by the Concord River. Thoreau's paragraph is a panegyric on the life of a boat man and continues on into another in which he recalls his boyhood excitement at seeing and going on board canal boats that ascended the Concord River, and were reported up the Sudbury as far as Fairhaven Bay. "We might say that our river was navigable,—why not?" Following this he celebrated commerce (that is, shipping) and ends with the verse, "Man's little acts are grand." In the fifteen lines of this verse, man's South Sea trade is celebrated and the picture, now shifted from canal boats to ocean ships, supports the rather astonishing and untranscendental statement that this is what ocean, sun, moon, and winds were made for![21]

The Middlesex Canal flourished in Thoreau's boyhood and brought Concordians many reminders that Boston's commerce stretched inland to them. Concord River was vital to it, as it furnished water where it crossed, at grade, at Billerica. The bar and other obstructions in the Concord were cleared away, and Concord, Massachusetts, became a real part of a transportation network within which both freight and passenger boats were operated. The Canal was officially closed in 1843, but it was not till 1852 that the last boat made passage.

Thoreau was acutely aware of these powerful maritime demands upon the local scene, including its farmers. Originally farmers teamed oak to the Medford Shipyard with oxen. Thoreau thought of the "difficulties which the farmer silently overcomes, who conveys the keel or mast of a man-of-war...to the nearest port, which would have defied the skill of a tribe of savages to overcome." His feelings, therefore, were mixed when he gazed at an oak tree. The "agony of strength" which he viewed "at Derby's" was "a grand object," yet a price was set on it "for ship-timber, for knees to make stiff the sides of ships against the Atlantic billows." He could not rid himself of the idea that "the farmer living far inland has not thought of plows and carts alone." He not only "gets out wood to burn, but ship-timber.... It is he who says, 'Ye shall become money to me.' It is in the woods and the farmer's yard that the vessel is first put upon the stocks."[22]

It was even so in Revolutionary times. Oak timbers from the woods near the Willard Family's old farm had gone into the hull of the famous ship *Constitution*, and sixty pairs of oars had been shaped in Daniel Taylor's shop near the Milldam for the whaleboats patrolling the Charles River.[23] Thus both history and contemporary life cast a web in which, like it or not, Thoreau was caught. The double aspect of the milieu of everyday life is further detected in numbers of land-sea doublets and other descriptive combinations, such as: "men plow and sail," "Land and sea should be infinitely wild," "the seacoast with its wrecks and the wilderness with its living and decaying trees," farm boys running off to sea and sailors proving to be only farm boys on ships, Wellfleet "best combines the country and the seaside," pine groves "like temples or like fleets," "youth may build or plant or sail," "earning his means as he went, before the mast and behind the plow," "so enterprised or sailed in some way" as to feel like new men though in old clothes, and so on.

It is easy to speculate that just in his daily life Thoreau got more than "a little salted."[24]

Captain Thoreau

Is it not more attractive to be a sailor than a farmer?

No wonder men love to be sailors...gubernators to a piece of wood.

Journal

III

Captain Thoreau

It was quite natural that Thoreau took to sailing. Skimming across the flooded Concord meadows where he had walked dry-shod the day before, Thoreau exulted in the wind and waves. "I sail with a smacking breeze today," he entered in his *Journal*, "and I fancy that I am a sailor on the ocean. It is an advantage that all towns do not possess." That was in May of 1854, fifteen years after the famous excursion on the Concord and Merrimack rivers. His records of and comments on sailing, of one kind or another, span his active life. He sailed his inland ocean with unfailing zest and constant stretch of the imagination. In fact and fancy he crossed his little main, beat up to windward, or lolled before the wind, coasting the ever-familiar, ever-strange shores and returning to port richly laden. Of a July afternoon when the whole landscape was glaucous, he wrote in his *Journal*, "Now, when the fashionable world goes to Saratoga, Nahant, or Newport, we frequent our oldest haunts with new love and reverence and sail into new ports with each fresh varnish of the air."[1]

Thoreau not only sailed (however clumsily), he worked at being sailor-like (however ostentatiously). His first recorded voyage (though doubtless by no means his very first) was taken on the first of August, 1836, during the year when he had rusticated himself from Harvard because of ill health. Four days later he wrote in high spirits to his classmate Charles Wyatt Rice:

> I have been manufacturing a sort of vessel in miniature, not a *eusselmon nea* as Homer put it, but a kind of oblong bread-trough. . . . The following is an extract from the logbook of the *Red Jacket*, Captain Thoreau:
>
> Set sail from the island—the island! how expressive!—reached Thayer's after a tedious voyage, having encountered a head wind during the whole passage—waves running mountains high, with breakers to leeward—however, arrived safe, and after a thorough outfit, being provided with extra cables, and a first-rate birch mainmast, weighed anchor at 3 p.m., August 1, 1836, N.S., wind blowing N.N.E.

> The breeze having increased to a gale, tack'd ship and prepared for emergencies. Just as the ship was rounding Point Dennis a squall struck her, under a cloud of canvas, which swept the deck. The aforesaid mast went by the board, carrying with it the only mainsail. The vessel being left at the mercy of the waves was cast ashore on Nashawtuck beach. Natives—a harmless, unoffensive race, principally devoted to agricultural pursuits—appeared somewhat astonished that a stranger should land so unceremoniously on their coast.
>
> Got her off at twenty minutes of four, and after a short and pleasant passage of ten minutes arrived safely in port with valuable cargo.[2]

Twenty-four years later, two years before he died, he entered in his *Journal* for mid-March a speaking passage which indicates his confirmed habit of sailing, as well as his icy inauguration of the season of 1860:

> 16th. The ice of the night fills the river in the morning, and I hear it go grating downward at sunrise. As soon as I can get it painted and dried, I launch my boat and make my first voyage for the year. . . . I taste a spring cranberry, save a floating rail, feel the element fluctuate beneath me, and am tossed bodily as I am in thought and sentiment. Than longen folk to gon on *voyages*. The water freezes on the oars. I wish to hear my mast crack and my rapt boat run on her side, so low her deck drinks water and her keel plows the air. . . . The ice has broken up and navigation commenced. We may set sail for foreign ports or expect the first arrival any day. . . . I make more boisterous and stormy voyages now than at any season. . . . . I vastly increase my sphere and experience by a boat.[3]

His "first voyage for the year." Thus it had been, we may assume, without much variation for most of the years between. The dawn of each new season was marked by his ritual resumption of sailing. We also know that Thoreau not only enjoyed sailing; he at times pondered the life of a sailor:

> Is it not more attractive to be a sailor than a farmer? The farmer's son is restless and wants to go to sea. Is it not better to plow the ocean than the land? In the former case the plow runs further in its furrow before it turns. You may go round the world before the mast, but not behind the plow.[4]

This spirit informs parts of the *Week*. Again, in a somewhat less ebullient remark as late as 1857, he ranks sailing with farming, building and manufacturing as "the wholesomest amusements that were ever invented."[5] And about two months later (January 1, 1858) he was writing to George Thatcher:

> I am glad to hear that Charles [Thatcher] has a good situation, but I thought that the 3rd mate lived with and as the sailors. If he makes a study of navigation &c, and is bent on being master soon, well & good. It is an honorable and brave life, though a hard one, and turns as good men as most professions. Where there is a good character to be developed, there are very few callings better calculated to develop it.

In the *Week* he records that, seeing some carpenters at work mending a scow, their mallets echoing from shore to shore as if they were "a-caulking the sky," he realized that "boat-building was as ancient and honorable an art as agriculture and that there might be a naval as well as a pastoral life. The whole history of commerce was made manifest in that scow turned bottom upward." And he exaggeratedly adds that it is better to build your own boat when you come to a stream, as the Indians did, than to have to depend on a ferry or bridge.[6]

The summers of 1852 and 1853 were especially pleasant for Thoreau the sailor. The pleasure of sailing was akin to that which a planet feels. "It seems a more complete adventure than a walk."[7] Continuing a comparison of riding and sailing, he added in a day or so, "I carry so many me's with me.... Our capacity to carry our furniture with us is so much increased. There is little danger of overloading the steed.... We embark; we go aboard a boat; we sit or stand.... If you have a cabin and can descend into that, the charm is double."[8]

Season after season this mood of pleasure and excitement continues. An especially interesting entry in his *Journal* is that for August 30, 1853:

> Set sail homeward about an hour before sundown. The breeze blows me glibly across Fair Haven, the last dying gale of the day. No wonder men love to be sailors, to be blown about the world sitting at the helm, to shave the capes and see the islands disappear under our sterns,—gubernators to a piece of wood. It disposes to contemplation, and is to me instead of smoking."[9]

Here we may note all the aspects of sailing that were important to Thoreau: the excitement of sailing itself with its attendant feeling of pleasure and sense of power, the celebration of the life of a sailor, and a certain resulting philosophic drift of mind anticipating that on the deck of Melville's *Pequod.* (It may, however, demand a certain tolerance to imagine a deepwater sailor *sitting* at the helm.) Thoreau had been sailing for years on the local rivers when he wrote the "gubernators" passage, and the lift which sailing gave to his spirit is on record for all to read in that gay, thoughtful, prolix book, *A Week on the Concord and Merrimack Rivers.*

A few passages in *Walden* and most of the *Week* may lead us somewhat too easily to assume that Thoreau's sailing was merely dreamful and fancy-breeding, an exercise conducive mainly to the free flow of transcendental analogies. However, a long passage in the entry of April 29, 1856, describes his physical and aesthetic pleasure and exhilaration. It is a brisk day when there is a good sea and plenty of sparkle on the water. The waves leap and roll like porpoises. They gurgle under the stern. He experiences "an agreeable sense" of sliding over and through them, bound on his own errands, while their motion is chiefly an undulation. The feeling of motion is intoxicating, "like the effect of wine." "It is flattering to a sense of power to make the wayward wind our horse and sit with our hand on the tiller. Sailing is much like flying, and from the birth of our race men have been charmed by it." Awe mixes with exhilaration on the roughest day which he records. The "black-backed waves" two feet high surge about him like "gamboling monsters of the deep.... They are *melainai*—what is the Greek for waves? This is our black sea.... Only one of the epithets which the poets have applied to the color of the sea will apply to this water,—*melaina, μέγαινα θάλασσα*. I was delighted to find that our usually peaceful river could toss me so. How much more exciting than to be planting potatoes with those men in the field! What a different world!" Beyond the bridge at last, he lay awhile in the smooth water and listened: "It sounded like the breakers on the seashore heard from *terra firma*."[10] This spirit of excitement never died. As late as 1859 he recorded, "Here...you scud before the wind in your tight bark and listen to the surge (or sough?) of the great waves sporting around you, while you hold the steering-oar and your mast bends to the gale and you stow all your ballast to windward."[11]

The association of the fresh inland water of the Concord world with the salt waters of mysterious and limitless oceans we have taken for granted, perhaps, since Emerson said in 1862: "To him there was no such thing as size. The pond was a small ocean; the Atlantic, a large Walden Pond." Not only the Pond, but every stream was a sea. In June of 1857 he wrote to Harrison Blake to "invite you men of Worcester to this quiet *Mediterranean* shore." Though it is not clear whether the proposed expedition was to climb mountains or sail rivers, Thoreau assured Blake that he would "be rejoiced" to see him "and to act the part of skipper in the contemplated voyage." He had already written in the *Week*:

> The smallest stream is *mediterranean* sea, a smaller ocean creek within the land, where men may steer by their farm bounds and cottage lights.... But for the geographers, I should hardly have known how large a portion of the globe is water, my life has chiefly passed within so deep a cove. Yet I have sometimes ventured as far as to the mouth of my Snug Harbor.[12]

Thoreau sailed for literally hundreds of miles on such mediterranean seas. The fame of the two-weeks journey *up* the Merrimac has obscured the fact that he may have sailed just as far *down*. When Hawthorne bought Thoreau's boat, the *Musketaquid*, in 1842, "Mr. Thorow's" fame as a sailor was for *down*. "It is not very likely," wrote Hawthorne, "that I shall make such long voyages in her as Mr. Thorow has done. He once followed our river down to the Merrimac, and thence, I believe, to Newburyport—a voyage of about eighty miles, in this little vessel."[13]

Thoreau was particularly impressed by the magic of extracting power from the wind, and the control of this power by the sailor. On both fresh and salt water this knowledge delighted him. "How much he knows of the wind, its strength and direction,whose steed it is,—the sailor." The most vivid lesson he learned in the control of the wind he learned in July of 1851 in the neighborhood of Duxbury and Plymouth where he went sailing many times, and where his adventures in a mackerel schooner opened his eyes.

> This sailing on the salt water was something new to me. The boat is such a living creature, even this clumsy one sailing within five points of the wind. The sailboat is an admirable invention, by which you compel the wind to transport you even against itself. . . . It is so contrary to expectation, as if the elements were disposed to favor you. This deep unfathomable sea! but this wind ever blowing over it to transport you![14]

No doubt his limp analogy in the Friday Section of the *Week* about "the best sailor" being one who sails within the fewest points of the wind would have been more concrete and meaningful if he had enjoyed his Plymouth experience beforehand.[15]

Quiet days also had their appeal, impressing him with the domestic aspect of sailing. It is pleasant to sail, he wrote on the last day of August 1852; the boat is your home for the day, a studio. "It is almost as if you put oars out at your windows and moved your house along. A sailor, I see, easily becomes attached to his vessel." In the rain with only an umbrella in the stern for a cabin, he "enjoyed the adventure because it combined to some extent the advantages of being at home in my chamber and abroad in the storm at the same time.[16]

Thoreau's pleasure and excitement from sailing never faded, and we may deduce from a number of remarks that his ideal small craft would be a cabin sloop. However, as in most other aspects of his economy, he got along with the simplest kind of craft, a small flat-bottomed skiff or dory with wooden tholepins, an easily stepped mast, and an oar for rudder.

No ship or boat of any kind or shape seemed to escape his eye. A journey to Maine brought him acquainted with bateaux and birch canoes. At Provincetown he could not get over the beauty and magnitude of the mackerel fleet. At Staten Island the most gratifying thing he did was to gaze seaward and count the ships in the Narrows. Journeys to these places were accomplished in part by sloops, packets, or steamers, during which parts of the journeys he duly recorded facts of nautical interest: the kind of ship, her name, how she sailed, her schedule, her captain, crew, and passengers. Any small boat had special meaning, and he often stopped to make sketches thereof. He and Channing spent one fall afternoon on the Concord discussing "boats of different patterns." These were the "dead-river boats, not to be matched by Boston carpenters,"

> punts, bread-troughs, flatirons, etc., etc. . . . water carriages of various patterns and in various conditions,—some for pleasure (against the gentleman's seat?); some for ducking, small and portable; some for honest fishing, broad and leaky but not cranky; some with spearing fixtures; some stout and square-endish for hay boats; one canal-boat or mud-scow in the weeds, not worth getting down the stream, like some vast pike that could swallow all the rest, proper craft for our river.[17]

Along the New Bedford shores he took note of the lines, construction, and especially the seaworthiness of whaleboats, with his customary references to flat-bottomed types like skiffs that were preferable for sailing the rivers and ponds of Concord.

When he sailed in the mackerel schooner out from Plymouth to Clark's Island, he felt that he had almost indeed been on a fishing cruise. He sat with the fishermen, helped to navigate the vessel, and at his destination had an attentive audience of men and boys to whom he told stories of the Vikings and exchanged anecdotes of the sea. It was on that excursion that he discovered the Atlantic short-haired harbor seals and wondered why no one had told him about them before. They furnished just the touch of wildness that made New England harbors completely meaningful.

> Singular that these strange animals should be so abundant here and yet the man who lives a few miles inland never heard of them. To him there is no report of the sea, though he may read the Plymouth paper. The Boston papers do not tell us that they have seals in the Harbor. The inhabitants of Plymouth do not seem to be aware of it. I always think of seals in connection with Esquimaux or some other outlandish people, not in connection with those who live on the shores of Boston or Plymouth harbors.[18]

It is only when we have read this passage that we are equipped to read a metaphorical remark a few days later apropos of stepping into the wild from civilization: "This is so easy and so common, though our literature implies that it is rare! We in the country make no report of the seals and sharks in our neighborhood to those in the city. We send them only our huckleberries, not wild free thoughts."[19] The passage introduces a long and important statement on traveling at home, the key sentence of which moved out into a significant place in *Walden*. Both the *Week* and *Walden* engage the idea that it takes a man of genius to travel in his own country, "to make any progress between his door and his gate." He marveled, therefore, that the people of Plymouth and Boston did not see their own world, did no "traveling" at home.

One great and almost continuous preoccupation with sailing is to be found in his reading of voyages, wherein he seemed to touch the intrepid, adventuring spirit of Man. Yet he was interested not only in the purpose and success of such voyages and voyagers, but in the working of their ships. He pored over manuals like R. H. Dana's *Seaman's Friend* where he learned about reef-knots and spritsails and gaff and boom rigs; and he read Enoch Wines' *Two Years and a Half in the Navy. . .on Board of the U.S. Frigate "Constellation"*, according to John Aldrich Christie,[20] "for its methodical introduction to every feature of a sailing vessel." Christie has identified 171 travel accounts read by Thoreau, 83 of which Thoreau refers to directly. Furthermore, Thoreau's library contained maps, atlases, coast surveys, and nautical almanacs as well as voyages and travels. And Thoreau's compelling interest in such things as the habits and measurements of waves, the unharnessed power of the tide, the erosion of continental shore lines, the formation of sand bars (concerning which he speculated a useful mathematical formula might be constructed), dust in the sea air, the influence of the moon on the tides, singing sands—all no doubt shared responsibility for his outcry in the summer of 1851 against the astringent force of cold scientific knowledge: "I fear that the character of my knowledge is from year to year becoming more distinct and scientific; that in exchange for views as wide as heaven's cope, I am being narrowed down to the field of the microscope. I see details, not wholes nor the shadows of wholes." But as if to show that he would never allow to be stifled his impulse to draw large analogies (in other words to be still in command), he wrote shortly thereafter, concerning the moon's influence upon the earth:

> Is not the poet who walks by night conscious of a tide in his thought which is to be referred to lunar influence, in which the ocean within him overflows its shores and bathes the dry land? Has he not his spring-tides and his neap-tides, the former sometimes combining with winds of heaven to produce those memorable high tides of the calendar which leave their marks for ages, when all Broad Street [Boston] is submerged, and incalculable damage is done to the ordinary shipping of the mind?[21]

Although impulses and insights may flow over him like a tide, Thoreau never intends to be mere flotsam. Some one must be in command of that "shipping of the mind."

As an image of control, the tiller was more attractive than the plow handle, even as any New England farm boy found the sea more alluring than the farm. Farm and sea were still the two dominant areas of man's daily activity in New England, despite the already developing streamside mills. As late as *Walking*, Thoreau shows this accepted division of the work world. One of his most famous remarks is reinforced by it. "Wilderness is the preservation of the world. Men plough and sail for it."[22] His easy familiarity with a nautical posture, furthermore, is to be noted in unexpected little places, as in the cock-crow passage near the end of *Walking* where he celebrates "the gospel according to this moment." He whose senses are alive and hears the cock crow in every barnyard "has not fallen astern."

We often observe Thoreau navigating the land. "Most of us are still related to our native fields as the navigator to undiscovered islands in the sea," he wrote. "We can any autumn discover a new fruit there which will surprise by its beauty or sweetness."[23] He was the Columbus of Concord—or perhaps its East Indiaman. The world was to him, over and over, a landfall to be sighted, a far shore to be reached, or a palm-decked island. Indeed, "far shore" became one of his richest metaphors.

In mountain climbing he found it most convenient "to steer by distant objects."[24] He constantly carried a compass, and he characteristically "steered a course" through the woods or along the hillsides, pausing occasionally to "get [his] bearings." This becomes figurative near the end of *Walden* where he writes, "I delight to come to my bearings,—not walk . . . with pomp and parade . . . but to walk even with the Builder of the universe."[25] The climax of the doggerel verse "The Old Marlborough Road" (in *Walking*) is the familiar quatrain:

If with fancy unfurled
  You leave your abode,
You may go round the world
  By the old Marlborough Road.

One of the most amusing and relaxed moments of walking-sailing appears in *Walden*. In "The Village" section Thoreau describes his cruise home to his Snug Harbor one night after a pleasant visit in Concord town:

> It was very pleasant, when I stayed late in town, to launch myself into the night, especially if it was dark and tempestuous, and set sail from some bright village parlor or lecture room, with a bag of rye or

> Indian meal upon my shoulder, for my snug harbor in the woods, having made all tight without and withdrawn under hatches with a merry crew of thoughts, leaving only my outer man at the helm, or even tying up the helm where it was plain sailing. I had many a genial thought by the cabin fire "as I sailed." I was never cast away nor distressed in any weather, though I encountered some severe storms.

The long paragraph goes on to discuss how he often traverses familiar ground with scarcely any awareness of the path or of familiar landmarks, and how valuable an experience it is to be lost in the woods. The paragraph is a model of that kind of artistic process by which the reader is easily led from the concreteness of the little narrative of homecoming, outward to the discussion of getting lost, and finally to the full significance to him of such an experience. The last three sentences not only present the transcendental paradox, but complete the nautical framework that helps to hold the paragraph nicely together:

> In our most trivial walks, we are constantly, though unconsciously, steering like pilots by certain well-known beacons and headlands, and if we go beyond our usual course we stll carry in our minds the bearing of some neighboring cape; and not until we are completely lost, or turned around...do we appreciate the vastness and strangeness of nature. Every man has to learn the points of compass again as often as he awakes, whether from sleep or abstraction. Not till we are lost, in other words not till we have lost the world, do we begin to find ourselves, and realize where we are and the infinite extent of our relations.

Quoting this as I have, it sounds more solemn than it really is. The gayety of the moment, too, should not escape us. Thoreau is not only a sailor sailing home; he is the pirate Captain Kidd. "I had many a genial thought by the cabin fire 'as I sailed,'" he says, knowing that his reader would recall the refrain of the famous and long-popular ballad of Captain Kidd. I have no doubt that he sang it and shouted a few orders to his crew.

Occasionally Thoreau identified the sailor with elemental man, or with whole societies of men. In *Cape Cod*, when he hears a young male passenger on the Hingham boat explaining to his companion the legend of the treacherous ledge, Nix's Mate, Thoreau observes that "it is the illiterate and unimaginative class that seizes on and transmits the legends in which the more cultivated delight. No fastidious poet dwelling in Boston had tampered with it,—no narrow poet, but broad mankind, sailors from all ports sailing by." In one sense the young cigar-smoking city boy is not sailor; yet as sailor sailing past the infamous ledge and repeating the tale, he is all untutored mankind.

It is not generally known that Thoreau's early word for that elemental, Homeric man, Therien the Canadian woodchopper, was "sailor-like." This fascinating half-wild man (in the Thoreauvian sense) is a good illustration of what Matthiessen (paraphrasing Thomas Mann) calls, "the mode of celebrating life whereby the moment becomes infinitely larger than itself, and the individual existence escapes from its narrow bounds and finds sanction and consecration."[26] Thoreau recognized in the woodchopper that "the uneradicated wildness of man is the anarchical basis both of all that is most dangerous and most valuable in him." This dualism he observed more than once in the life and character of sailors. So it is that his first description of Therien is: "One a handsome younger man a sailor-like-Greek-like man says to me today—'Sir, I like your notions—I think I shall live so myelf. Only I should like a wilder country.'"[27]

Thus Thoreau found the figure of man sailing a more interesting and a more relevant representation of qualities he cherished than that of the farmer. It was a psychic kinship with the sailor's relation to free and open space, his mobility, and his sense of command and direction. Readers of the Conclusion to *Walden* know that Thoreau's figure for meditative thought is sailing the inner sea. The ancient precept "Know thyself" becomes in Thoreau "Explore thyself." And he means to evoke the figure of the grand navigator sailing to unknown worlds. Let every man be his own Columbus and sail the inner seas of thought.

As traveler, Thoreau was frequently a sailor. As traveler to distant places, outward or inward, he can be counted on to sail. His whole life was a voyage. He was captain of his own life, as few men have ever been. In more ways than one he was "Captain Thoreau," studying home-cosmography, gubernator to himself.

The World as Symbol

My thought is a part of the meaning of the world, and hence I use a part of the world as a symbol to express my thought.

Journal

He is the richest who has most use for nature as raw material for tropes and symbols with which to describe his life.

Journal

IV

The World as Symbol

THE MARITIME COLORING of Thoreau's world was inescapable. Thoreau saw clearly its outlines and sensed its vitality. He felt its stretched power, heard and spoke some of its common language, read dozens of its books, and in his middle and later years pondered the mysteries and meanings of the sea along the shore and in America's crowded harbors from New York to Bangor. As he went to the wharves and open stretches of the Atlantic seashore, some of his youthful hearsay knowledge and vocabulary was sharpened by first-hand observation. He journeyed energetically and often. He looked and listened as acutely away from Concord and with the same poetic and philosophical monitors as those he employed in the pastoral Concord vicinity. This is precisely what is encompassed by Emerson's well known remark that he "carried Concord with him" wherever he went.

Most immediately obvious in his marine language was a jocose, affected vocabulary. In keeping with his love of linguistic playfulness and of over-statement (his "extra-vagance") he paraded salty terms. He amused himself by taking pains to repeat words like "luff," "bear away," "belay," "closehaul," and "standing out," which last phrase he admitted he rather liked.[1] He not only built a crude boat; he built a nautical vocabulary about as heavy as his boat. The foolery in the log of the "*Red Jacket*, Captain Thoreau" is an excellent example. The light linguistic touch in the *Week*, however, is directed to a more controlled and poetic end. Linguistic exaggeration there helps to swell that simple boating trip into an ocean odyssey of significant intent. The river towns are "havens," "ports," "harbors," and "roadsteads." The Thoreau brothers do not launch their clumsy boat from its actual grassy mooring in the mud where it was chained to a tree; they "weigh anchor." Camp sites are "snug harbors." Leaving Salmon Brook they "stand out" to sea again, and Thoreau comments on the robustness of the phrase. The river banks are "coasts." Points of land are characteristically "capes" and distant "headlands." Both the freshets and the normal flow of water are "tides." In their heavy bread-trough of a boat the Merrimac navigators imagine they are deep water sailors, and every leg of the trip is a "voyage." "Here was that 'pleasant harbor' we had sighed for where the weary voyageur could read the journal of some other sailor, whose bark had ploughed, perchance, more famous and classic seas," he writes on Tuesday.

This surfeit of nautical metaphors (sometimes mixed with others just as familiar)[2] is probably the longest extended illustration of that melange of wry exaggeration and seriousness for which Thoreau is either applauded or condemned. His *Journal* is an intermittent further record of his poetic and stylistic experiments with them. In accordance with his own theory that one sees what he is already carrying in his mind, these moments effectively indicate how susceptible his mind was in this little observed area of experience. Talking to himself, as it were, he noted on October 2, 1858 that frogs release themselves from the mud, float to the surface, then "let go all, drop anchor." He wrote to Harrison Blake in November of '57, concerning a non-existent mountain of which he dreamed, "I keep a mountain anchored off eastward a little way, which I ascend in my dreams both awake and asleep." The creaking of his oars sounded "like a block in a harbor, such a sound as would bring tears to an old sailor's eyes. It suggests to me adventure and seeking one's fortune..."[3]—a reflection doubtless of his early romantic yearnings as he stood on Long Wharf and watched the sails go creaking up and the ships slipping gracefully down Boston Harbor. For convenience, we may group these far from rare and random figures as follows for their rhetorical and philosophical significance: 1) the playful, the striking and the unexpected, 2) the revitalizing of stale metaphor, 3) the oft repeated favorite image, 4) the significant (or confusing) figure that is made more clear when the maritime aspect is known, 5) the intrusive maritime figure that lives with others and sometimes dominates in a group, and 6) the figure used to vivify something of profound importance to Thoreau. The task is to catch a glimpse of Thoreau as that "richest" person who made most use of some of the now little observed "raw material" of one pervading aspect of life around him "for tropes and symbols with which to describe his life."

At the risk of tedious gathering of too many instances, one may profitably note a few examples from the private world of his journals and letters. Take the odd association of insects and weed seeds with a ship's rigging. Doubtless few people would think of beggar lice or grasshoppers in nautical terms. On August 19, 1856 Thoreau walked through a particularly thick growth of "these desmodiums...so fine and inobvious," putting chains around him like savage children. "They escape your observation, as it were under bare poles. You notice only as far up as their green sails are set, perchance, or to the crosstrees, not the tall, tapering raking spars, whence are looped the life lines and halyards. Or it is like that slanting mast and rigging in navy-yards.... I saw the other day a cricket standing on his head in a chocolate-colored (inside) fungus, only his tail-yards visible."[4] The flooded meadows of August '56 drove grasshoppers and caterpillars up the stalks of grass and weeds "to take refuge in the rigging." Some stalks had seven or eight grasshoppers "clinging to their masts...like shipwrecked sailors now the third or fourth day exposed. Whither shall they jump? It is a quarter of a mile to the shore, and countless sharks lie in wait for them." The next day he notes that swallows are skimming over the flooded meadows. "Are they catching the grasshoppers as they cling to bare poles?"[5] These grasshoppers-as-sailors are not inversions of the familiar nineteenth-century figure of sailors spry as grass-hoppers "jumping from spar to spar" (as Melville's Ishmael describes them). They derive from the graphic description of desperate men clinging to the rigging which Thoreau at one time got first hand (and reported in *Cape Cod*). A carpenter had saved himself that way when the ill-fated lumber schooner on which he had been sailing to Boston from Maine but a few days before had to be beached by running head on into the boiling surf in the same storm that had wrecked the emigrant-laden brig *St. John*. In the wreck of the schooner all lives were saved, and the unexcitable fur-capped Maine carpenter came off a wiser man: "I held on to the running rigging, but I have learned to hold on the standing rigging next time."[6]

A loping calf was like a ship in a rough sea, but so also was a loping boy. In the Friday section of the *Week* there is an amusing little picture of a farm boy "let loose" to go to the County Fair. "The wind goes hurrying down the country, gleaning every loose straw...left in the fields, while every farmer lad too appears to scud before it, having donned his best pea-jacket and pepper-and-salt waistcoat, his unbent trousers, outstanding rigging of duck or kerseymere or corduroy, and his furry hat withal...."[7] This *al fresco* vignette shades off into a wholly sympathetic description of rural people at the Fair worthy of, and indeed suggesting, the amused humanity of an urbane Charles Lamb. The farm boy as sailor reverses that other picture of bustling humanity on Long Wharf where seafarers look like misplaced farmers. The richness of these observations related directly to the tradition (as Dana tells us) of calling raw sailors—fresh from their farm—"boys," no matter what their age, once they had signed aboard a ship before the mast.

Thoreau often added nautical details to bring to life what might otherwise be a stale metaphor. His use of the verb "launch" is an instance. He was thoroughly familiar with the majestic and complicated event of a ship launching, a kind of birth trauma fraught with beauty and danger. Precariously high on her cradle, the ship had to be raised by blocks and sent down the slippery ways into safe deep water. When he once complained of facile journalists, he wrote, "But the reviewer seizes his pen and shouts, 'Forward! Alamo and Fanning!' Immediately the author discovers himself launched, and if the slope is easy and the grease good, does not go to the bottom."[8] So much for a little picture of a chatting journalist. Regarding his own chanticleer-like utterance, he wrote very early, "When I utter a thought I launch a vessel which never sails in my haven more, but goes sheer off into the deep."[9]

There is no group of figures better than the nautical to illustrate Thoreau's well-recognized penchant for concreteness (see Emerson's remark). Large open spaces around Concord of land or water, in either summer or winter, are seas. Over and over, he describes the meadows as the "green Sea," which is hardly a lively or original metaphor inasmuch as tall grass or grain waving in the wind suggests to any mind waves on water. The figure of a meadowy sea, furthermore, may owe something to Humboldt's *Narrative*, as Christie suggests. Thoreau, however, extends, renews, and saves the image by keeping it strictly local, and personal, as when he stood in sedge grass on J. P. Brown's land and recorded that he felt he was "navigating," and the waves were "hastening to break on the shore."[10] Or at another time in another field he felt "a little as if caught by a rising tide on flats far from the shore. . . cast away in the midst of the sea," yet gazing "toward the distant mainland."[11] Just after returning from a trip to New Bedford, his eye swept a broad Concord meadow, and he saw "shadows of clouds on it as on the sea."[12] The meadow remained a sea even in winter when it was covered up. One day when he had skated thirty miles, he warns that "the deep dark channel between sunken willow rows" must be crossed with caution, for it is best to remember that the willows separate this partly open channel "from the meadowy sea."[13] On another winter day he found himself returning on the ice "over a green sea, winding amid purple islets. . . a smooth green sea, or *aequor*."[14] In February of 1855 (a good month that year for skating) he adapted from Landor's *Richard the First* a sailing fantasy of his own, "past the old kingdoms of my fancy. . . the realms of my family," substituting local place names for European.[15]

Sometimes the nautical intrudes in a scene controlled by another figure, as in the description of Sam Barrett's Mill. "Am pleased to see the cobweb drapery of the mill. Each fine line hanging in festoons. . . is covered and greatly enlarged by a coating of meal. . . like tassels and tapestry of a counterpane. . . . It is as if I were aboard a man-of-war, and this were the fine 'rigging' of the mill, the sails being taken in."[16] Another instance of this is the famous battle of the ants in *Walden*, where the nautical image is likely to be taken only as a familiar well-worn phrase. The main figure evokes a field of heroic battle, with military language and mention of Achilles and his Myrmidons elevating it to Homeric scale, red and black in mortal combat. "The smaller red champion had fastened himself like a vise to his adversary's front, and through all the tumblings on that field never for an instant ceased to gnaw at one of his feelers near the root, having already caused the other to go by the board." The metaphors are mixed, yet the last phrase is strikingly fitting. Though *to go by the board* has been tamely glossed as meaning "to fall overboard," it really means here, as it did on ships in Thoreau's day, that the destroyed feeler has the heroic dimension of a ship's tall mast that has broken at the base and crashed in a tangle of wreckage. A similar poetic extension comes from using a single word which dramatically refocuses a simple scene. Describing a pine grove: "How the winds roared among the shrouds of the wood."[17] With a single word *shrouds* the pine grove bcomes a ship at sea in a gale, its masts well guyed by the slanting ladderlike shrouds and the whole ship alive with the howl of the wind through these major features of the rigging.

Thoreau was moved by the whole creative act of shipbuilding. He once observed a man making a violin. "I have seen a man making himself a viol, patiently and fondly paring the thin wood and shaping it, and when I considered the end of the work he was ennobled in my eyes. He was building himself a ship in which to sail to new worlds." This was written in a *Journal* passage (II, 72) that sprang from hearing a neighbor singing and then in observing the salutary effect of all music on man. Thoreau's sensitivity here to the art of ship-building and to the ship as an example of architectural process, paring and shaping wood according to a conceived plan, matches his eulogy of ship-building in the *Week*. The idea of ship-building as a long and worthy process connected with ancient time and ancient skill is most eloquently suggested in the Spring section of *Walden*, where the great age and wisdom of the old man who saw the ice go out of Fair Haven Pond are described in this expansive figure: "One old man, who has been a close observer of Nature, and seems as thoroughly wise in regard to all her operations as if she had been put on the stocks when he was a boy, and he had helped to lay her keel...told me...."[18]

This tribute to the creative act of shipbuilding places Thoreau among those of his time who, like Whitman, Dana, Emerson, and Horatio Greenough, not only saw the beauty of the American sailing ship but understood its indigenous character, a contemporary example of an art form which had evolved from the homely functions and needs of daily life. It was the "huge-hull'd clean-shap'd New York clipper" that first stirred Whitman to write a poem. Emerson's remark that "the modern architecture is ship building," Matthiessen observes, led the architect Greenough to his eloquent celebration of the majestic American "ship at sea" as the kind of thing that might be designed in civil as well as naval architecture.[19] In *Cape Cod*, Thoreau wrote, "Perhaps we have reason to be proud of our naval architecture and need not go to the Greeks, or the

Goths, or the Italians, for models of our vessels." He was complaining that sea captains of Brewster, whose vessels were so good, should live in flimsy "Cambridgeport" houses that were so bad.[20]

The measure of Thoreau's sensitiveness to ships, however, lies not merely in his statements about them. He had seen many varieties of ships in American harbors and off the coast, both singly and in fleets and stately processions. Like Ishmael at the Battery, he did his share of water-gazing from the edges of many busy harbors from Bangor to New York. And since the day he built his first boat and recognized the kinship of a boat to a fish (below the waterline) and to a bird (above the waterline), relationships suggested by wind and water made it an easy step to further analogies.

The first ship image in Thoreau's *Journal* appears in his entry for December 19, 1837, at the end of a paragraph describing ice crystals on the Concord River. At first they suggest some sort of mosaic work, then they are prisms, and finally they "resembled the roofs and steeples of a Gothic city, or the vessels of a crowded haven under press of canvas." Thoreau had not yet been to Plymouth or Provincetown. He was doubtless thinking at that time of Boston Harbor where he knew schooners and squareriggers often were held in the Harbor waiting for good weather. However, after he had seen the Provincetown mackerel fleet—one of the most impressive sights at Cape Cod, judging from the number of times Thoreau recalled the event—that fleet supplied a favorite image for mass phenomena, merging with details from his harbor image. Boston and Salem and New Bedford sent ships to the remotest parts of the world; Provincetown fished in its own back yard. The entire town was absorbed in this one act; and Thoreau said he had never seen such a completely maritime community, though we know that by the time he composed his *Cape Cod*, he had been in Salem and Gloucester. The fleet was Provincetown's grand institution, lively, native, picturesque. Thoreau never forgot it. In the early morning the schooners sailed out to the fishing grounds, fished the schools of mackerel offshore where found, often plainly visible from the backside of the Cape. At night they "poured around" Race Point into the harbor and anchored, "a kind of society" arranged in a natural formation and moving on a time schedule dictated by their function. These graceful and serviceable two-masters stirred Thoreau's mind, as well they might, being upwards of 1500 craft he was told by an old fisherman. Thoreau himself counted two hundred in the harbor at one time. He saw them like fowls flying out and returning to roost, or like moths hovering about a candle. Many pages in *Cape Cod* are devoted to them, and they are the last visual impression he had of the Cape, as the packet bore him back to Boston across the Bay when the Cape itself was already "hull down." This "hull down" image itself was to furnish the dramatic climax to a long, imposing, and nautically swelled paragraph in the "Conclusion" to *Walden.*

The high point of the operation of the mackerel fleet, both practically and aesthetically, was their mass maneouvering while fishing. "Though their sails were set, they never sailed away, nor yet came to anchor," Thoreau notes, but they tacked as close together as "vessels in a haven." At first he thought they were contending with head winds but soon learned that they were fishing, and that they fished without lowering their sails. He counted 80 to 100 together at the same time. Just as birds and moths helped him describe this canvas society, so when he was back in Concord, the mackerel fleet came to mind several times when he watched flocks of yellow butterflies; and all of the many later descriptions of masses of triangular ice crystals (with one exception) are "whole fleets of shining sails" or "like a fleet of a thousand mackerel-fishers under press of sail careering before a smacking breeze."

One passage on clouds in the *Journal* indicates how his mind could pull back from an image of an East Indiaman to the apparently irresistible one of that Provincetown fleet. "The drifting, white downy clouds are to the landsmen what sails on the sea are to him that dwells by the shore, objects of a large, diffusive interest.... They are the flitting sails in that ocean whose bounds no man has visited.... We know no Ternate nor Tidore grand enough whither we can imagine them bound.... They are among the most glorious objects in nature. A sky without clouds is a meadow without flowers, a sea without sails. Some days we have the mackerel fleet."[21]

The schooner itself, indigenous as the huckleberry, seemed to Thoreau "the typical vessel."[22] He was so familiar with the schooner rig that it came as a surprise to read in "Dana"(R. H. Dana's *The Seaman's Friend*, a copy of which he owned) that there was another fore-and-aft sail, the spritsail, a rig in which the sail is extended away from the mast by a single diagonal "boom or gaff." Thoreau's gratuitous notation ends, "most fore-and-aft sails have [both] a gaff and a boom."[23]

Thoreau often saw trees as ships. His favorite trees were oaks and pines. The warmth of feeling he had for the white pine, evident wherever he wrote poetically about it, is seen dramatically in his first article on the Maine woods submitted to the young *Atlantic Monthly,* where he spoke of "the living spirit of the tree." Injudiciously (for his time) he concluded: "it is as immortal as I am, and perchance will go to as high a heaven, there to tower above me still." Editor James Russell Lowell, as the world well knows, silently cut out the sentence and thereby drew fire from Thoreau in a scorching letter of protest. Singly and in masses, shining with light, and darkened in the woods, pines never failed to stir Thoreau. Sometimes at Walden he "rambled to pine groves standing like temples, or like fleets at sea, full-rigged, with wavy boughs, and rippling with light." The tallest pine on record, he gathered from the great French botanist Michaux, measured 180 feet. Just as oaks frequently suggested the tough knees and beams for ships, so the tall white pines in New England meant masts. The cutting of the forests of Maine and New Hampshire for the King's Navy was still fresh in the public memory. An eloquent passage in the *Journal* describes the cutting of a 200-year old 100-foot veteran which, though it was to be cut up for mill logs, was to him a "raking mast,—the hill its hulk." The burnt forests on the side of one of the PeterboroughHills were "tall bleached masts still standing." Eight years later some lopsided, wind-beaten black spruces atop Mt. Monadnock reminded him "often of masts of vessels with sails set on one side, and sometimes one of the almost bare masts is seen to have broken short off at ten feet from the ground. . . ."[24]

From the days when the King's mark reserved the tall pines of Maine and New Hampshire for the British navy, New Englanders had called them "masts" and "sticks." Once Thoreau was so excited when "two enormous pine sticks" were rushing by through the town on the railroad cars bound for the "Portsmouth Navy-Yard" that he ran (too late) to fetch his sister Sophia just to see them go by.[25] Readers of the "Sounds" section of *Walden* will recognize in this passage the first item in the list of things the railroad brings *down*. In *Walden*, however, certain familiar and colloquial effects (Sophia and the "two enormous pine sticks") have been dropped in favor of more elegant effects ("to be the mast/ Of some great admiral"). At Walden in the midst of a mixed grove of trees, "the shrines" he "visited both summer and winter," there might be "some taller mast of a pine." The tall pine, the tall ship.

His association of ships and trees extended to the hills and mountains themselves, with their dark masses of forest covering. "To seagoing men the very mountains are but boats turned upside down." He celebrated the "Delectable Mountains" he saw by looking west from Concord, in his long poem, "With Frontier Strength Ye Stand Your Ground." The whole first section is molded round the figure of a fleet of ships. At first the mountains are a naval convoy, but they emerge at the end as broad-beamed merchant ships fit for the *western* (Calfornia) trade, or anything else.

Like some vast fleet,
Sailing through rain and sleet,
Through winter's cold and summer's heat;
Still holding on upon your high emprise,
Until ye find a shore amid the skies;
Not skulking close to land,
With cargo contraband,

For they who sent a venture out by ye
Have set the Sun to see
Their honesty.
Ships of the line, each one,
Ye westward run,
Convoying clouds,
Which cluster in your shrouds,
Always before the gale,
Under a press of sail,
With weight of metal all untold,—
I seem to feel ye in my firm seat here,
Immeasurable depth of hold,
And breadth of beam, and length of running gear.
Methinks ye take luxurious pleasure
In your novel western leisure;
So cool your brows and freshly blue
As Time had naught for ye to do;
For ye lie at your length,
An unappropriated strength,
Unhewn primeval timber,
For knees so stiff, for masts so limber;
The stock of which new earths are made,
One day to be our *western* trade,
Fit for the stanchions of a world
Which through the seas of space is hurled.

Carl Bode's textual notes[26] indicate the great pains Thoreau took in the composition of this poem, pausing over expansions and rejections of nautical imagery. The whole 99-line poem is an exhibition of Thoreau's manipultaion of a simple ship metaphor, turning it this way and that as if in changing light, working it toward the ultimate theme of the west and the wild and the entire world moving in space. It is an early version of his "Homeric India man."

No less impressive is the nautical imagery that imaginatively shapes and gives significance to the oak leaf in "Autumnal Tints," Thoreau's last work.[27] In that essay—which ends with a kind of field-and-stream philosophy of aesthetics with stress on the visual—Thoreau reminds us that we see what we are prepared for, find what we search for. Under the influence of William Gilpin's writings on the picturesque (recently encountered), and also no doubt reminded at times by the living presence of his sister Sophia in his boat bound up the Assabet River with him to make sketches, Thoreau is induced to see pictures and landscape when he looks at fallen leaves or masses of blazing trees. His language here and there in the essay (especially in his description of reds) takes on the vocabulary of pictorial art. He speaks not only of "autumn tints" and "painted leaves" but paints, paint boxes, the nomenclature of colors, design, contrasts, relation of parts, perspective, picture, and frames. This shift from a concern with pleasure-giving single colors in individual species to masses and designs as in a landscape, is presented at the end of his Scarlet Oak section in the most vivid leaf description he ever wrote. It is accomplished with emphatic nautical images, chief of which is that of the shore, which philosophically was as meaningful as any that he brought forth.

The oak was Thoreau's favorite deciduous tree; the scarlet oak leaf his favorite leaf. Viewing this leaf, he indulges his imagination and creates a prose poem in its praise. He sees it first alive and at the top of the tree as an aerial dancer. Dead, dry, and fallen, it is like scrap tin cut by a die. It is a type from nature's font. The mind is "embayed" in its deep scallops. This seems to send his mind back to the short illustrated entry in his *Journal* for November 11, 1858.[28] Here a half dozen sentences on the silhouette of the scarlet oak leaf envision it as a heavily indented ocean shore offering deep bays and havens for mariners and propose it as a form worth an art student's copying in order to gain firmness of outline. In "Autumnal Tints" Thoreau expands the nautical details considerably, proposes two points of view, and keeps the whole close to his original idea of the leaf as design. It is his last rhetorical flare before he lifts his eye from the single leaf to the red and green forest garden a quarter of a mile away. He notes with pleasure the leaf's outline and how much richer it appears than "that, with its half dozen deep scallops, in which the eye and thought of the beholder are embayed." He compares it to a pond with rounded promontories, bays extending inland and narrowing into streams, "almost a leafy archipelago." But the most meaningful analogy he saves for last:

> But oftener it suggests land, and, as Dionysius and Pliny compared the form of the Morea to that of the leaf of the Oriental Planetree, so this leaf reminds me of some fair wild island in the ocean, whose extensive coast, alternate rounded bays with smooth strands, and sharp-pointed rocky capes, mark it as fitted for the habitation of man, and destined to become a centre of civilization at last. To the sailor's eye, it is a much-indented shore. Is it not, in fact, a shore to the aerial ocean, on which the windy surf beats? At the sight of this leaf we are all mariners, if not vikings, buccaneers, and filibusters. Both our love of repose and our spirit of adventure are addressed. In our most casual glance, perchance, we think that if we succeed in doubling those sharp capes we shall find deep, smooth, and secure

> havens in the ample bays. How different from the White-Oak leaf, with its rounded heads, on which no lighthouses need be placed! That is an England, with its long civil history, that may be read. This is some still unsettled New-found Island or Celebes. Shall we go and be rajahs there?

The answer is yes. On to new shores and new and richer lives where we may be not only rajahs of ourselves but founders of new civilizations. It is a familiar Thoreauvian idea. Among the pairs of symbolic opposites presented in the long, leaf metaphor (land and water, the sharp and the rounded, repose and adventure, etc.) the central and significant one involves social challenge. It excites Thoreau because it suggests the ever-present possibility of the new and renewable. The fair wild leaf-island repeats an idea, recurrent in his writing from at least 1843, of the symbolic importance of the seashore. This calls now for a more extended examination.

The Two Seas and the Shore

There was a time when the beauty and the music were all within, and I sat and listened to my thoughts, and there was a song in them...a positive, though faint and distant music, not sung by any bird, nor vibrating any earthly harp....I lay on the rocks, foundered like a harp on the seashore....You sat on the earth as on a raft, listening to music that was not of the earth, but which ruled and arranged it. Man *should be* the harp articulate.

Journal

Perhaps we should be equally mariners and terreners.

Paradise (to be) Regained

Thus we are amused with foam, a hybrid between two elements.... The debatable ground between two oceans, the earth or shore being the only point of resistance, where they are held to mingle.

Journal

V

The Two Seas and the Shore

THOREAU CUSTOMARILY SPEAKS of two oceans: the tidal salt waters of the globe and the "aerial sea." He responded as one would expect to the apparent boundlessness, fluid motion, and masked power of sea and air. In addition, certain specific and poetical aspects of both moved him: graceful craft navigating, surf and sounds of surf, and seascapes duplicated in morning fogs scanned from some high place where the air is seen and felt as a more volatile sea. The special physical and psychic point of reference for both seas is the shore—a vital, persistent, and revealing symbol.

Thoreau's universal shore represented a functional relationship with the sea rather than a containing lip or fine line of demarcation. He viewed the sea either as a landsman from the shore or, like a landsman turned sailor, amidst waves that roll and winds that blow toward some mystic shore that should be eagerly sought or chosen for a home. Either way, the shore was a point of focus and emphasis. Literally, he felt indigenous on the Atlantic littoral. Figuratively, he never stood anywhere else than on some shore. Philosophically, he felt the power and the perplexity of living along an earthly borderline between things higher and things lower, and like Willa Cather's archbishop he knew that lived on "the bright edges of the world."

This complex symbol of man's proper place did not always portray a fixed abode. It could be a point of departure or a point of arrival. In its completest sense it seems to represent the periphery of man's consciousness. It is a standing and a moving, a receiving of influence and a reaching out toward ultimate sources. In 1854, in his agony over waning poetic powers and the recollection of the time when joy, creativeness, and song reverberated throughout his being, he admits that he now lay "foundered like a harp on the seashore."[1] As harps are not normally marine flotsam, the strange figure has meaning only when we understand Thoreau's shore, the relationship of sea to shore, and Thoreau's yearning to be responsive like a harp to divine winds. In turn, it is through this figure—as well as others, as we shall see—that we are able to understand more clearly Thoreau's attempts to explore and express the complexities of man's philosophical being.

Thoreau's two seas are really one, symbols of various aspects of spiritual experience available to the earnest walker on the shore, and sought by the daring navigator of the sea. Though his major published writing (including the *Journal*) furnish numerous instances of his symbolic magnifying of the concept of the sea and the shore, no remark focuses the fact more sharply than a paragraph in his early review of J.A. Etzler's *Paradise Within the Reach of All Men*, in which he calls for more "mariner" qualities in us to mix with and balance off our "terrener" qualities.

> We have often thought that the fittest locality for a human dwelling was the edge of the land, that there the constant lesson and impression of the sea might sink deep into the life and character of the landsman, and perhaps impart a marine tint to his imagination. It is a noble word, that mariner, one who is conversant with the sea. There should be no more of what it signifies in each of us.... Perhaps we should be equally mariners and terreners, and even our Green Mountains need some of that sea-green to be mixed with them.[2]

In the carefully wrought passage on the scarlet oak leaf with which we ended the last chapter, we remember that Thoreau linked the sea and the shore in precisely this relationship. The bays and strands and capes outlined by the leaf's edge "mark it as fitted for the habitation of man...a shore to the aerial ocean.... At the sight of this leaf we are all mariners."

The figurative shore thus had the double advantage of facing the sea, with the sea's wide scope and ceaseless motion, and of facing not only the land but the space itself, with its even wider scope. An individual man may walk the beach at Cape Cod and put all America at his back, but also earthling man wherever he stands is on a shore with the whole earth at his back. Ahead lies the sea; wherever his feet are planted is a shore. Thus a seacoast, a tree, a mountain, a ship, a prairie, and even the sea itself may be a shore. A plowed upland field made him think, "seashore, earth-shore." Going up to Stow's young-oak woodland one winter day in 1859, Thoreau listened to the dry rustle of withered leaves that still held on. "It sounds like the roar of the sea, and is enlivening and inspiriting like that, suggesting how all the land is seacoast to the aerial ocean. It is the sound of the surf, the rut of an unseen ocean, billows of air breaking on the forest.... It rises and falls, wells and dies away, with agreeable alternation as the sea surf does." The universal backgrounds of sound "are essentially one voice, the earth-voice.... The earth is our ship, and this is the sound of the wind in her rigging as we sail."[3] Earth-bound man, walking his shores or sailing his seas, skirts the edge of the infinite, and all things both finite and infinite are instinct with meanings. They beat upon the consciousness of man.

The number and frequency of the jottngs in the *Journal* testify to the persistence of Thoreau's image of the atmosphere as an aerial sea. "The tiny bee," a great "voyager," rises over the top of the wood "and sets sail with his sweet cargo straight for his distant haven." If the luna moth ventures abroad by day, "some bird will pick out the precious cargo and let the sails and rigging drift, as when the sailor meets with a floating spar and sail and reports a wreck." A Harvard entomologist not long before had told Thoreau he had seen only the wings of a large emperor moth flutter down into the College Yard. "The wreck of an argosy in the air," adds Thoreau. A distant thunderhead fitfully flashing with lightning seemed "like a ship firing broadsides." Clouds and stars as sea isles are common. The ring of the toad in spring, when "Bufo the First" ascends to his throne, is "a sound from amid the waves of the aerial sea, that breaks on our ears with the surf of the air." Wind beating on the pines is likewise "like the surf on countless beaches, an endless shore."[4] This is a dependable, recurring figure for the music of the pines. Rarely in Thoreau do pines whisper or sigh.

Other sounds break like surf. The unpleasant associations aroused by the sound of church bells which Thoreau enlarges upon with such feeling in the Sunday section of the *Week* (the sound "breaking on these shores") originate in a brief essay-paragraph very early in the *Journal* on the same subject, where the Sabbath bell's "farthest waves are at this moment breaking on the cliffs." For the revised remark in the *Week* he preferred "shores" to "cliffs."

The most extreme display of aerial marine metaphor appears in the *Week* where the lethargy of the summer noon persuades the young Thoreau that all creatures then resign themselves "to float upon the inappreciable tides of nature." The thirteen-line poem which follows, *Woof of the Sun, Etherial Gauze*, is little more than a column of metaphors, more than half of which merely catalogue marine aspects.

Aerial surf upon the shores of earth,
Etherial estuary, frith of light,
Breakers of air, billows of heat,
Fine summer spray on inland seas.[5]

For twenty years such images amused and stimulated Thoreau, and he sometimes adopted odd angles of approach and points of viewing, including the sub-marine. "Would not snow-drifts be a good study, their philosophy and poetry?" he asked in January, 1852. "They are a sort of ripple-marks which the atmospheric sea makes on the snow-covered bottom." And two months later, gazing at some interesting clouds, he added, "Thus as the fishes look up at the waves, we look up at the clouds."

Readers before me have been struck by Thoreau's frequent descriptions of fog. He liked to extend and complicate the idea of fog as a sea. Looking from Fair Haven Hill at sunrise on July 25, 1852 he found it "a perfect sea...the tops of the higher hills are seen as islands, great bays...many miles across where the largest fleets would find ample room." Round Hill was "like a low sand-bar," the Wayland Hills "make a sort of promontory or peninsula like some Nahant.... I think of sea monsters that swim in the sea and of wrecks that strew the bottom, many a fathom deep." The Bedford meeting-house rising above the fog looked like a ship "with all sails set." He would sail the fog if he had "the right kind of bark, over to Annersack! for there she lies four miles from land as sailors say." Fog could seem more violent than the ocean itself. Looking from Nawshawtuct Hill he saw an ocean after "some tremendous and unheard of storm." "The seashore exhibits nothing more grand or on a larger scale.... It is as boundless as the view from the highlands of Cape Cod...exaggerated billows, the ocean on a larger scale." The actual sea, he insisted, "never appears so tossed up and universally white with foam and spray...where mountain billows are breaking on some hidden reef or bank.... It is tossed into the most boisterous seas, which no craft, no ocean steamer, is vast enough to sail on." In the poem, "Fog," the fog flows from ocean to sky, from sea to land, from sky to meadow. In the meager ten lines he crowds in eleven metaphors, the most vivid of which is the fog as a grounded ship: the fog is earth-bound.

Descended cloud fast anchored to the earth
That drawest too much air for shallow coasts.[6]

This "oceans of birds," as he several times calls the atmosphere, does however support a thriving aerial traffic. Emerging from the fog, the shrike (in the poem of that name) "his steady sails he never furls." It is safe to say that all large birds Thoreau, at one time or another, considered vessels maneuvering on the sea. Any one who has access to Francis Allen's *Notes on New England Birds* (1910), gathered from Thoreau's *Journal*, can quickly inform himself of this fact. The great herring gull flapping along "in the eye of a storm" is not able to hold "a steady course," but suddenly dashes upward "even like the surf of the sea." Or it beats up the river against the wind "tacking its way along like a sailing vessel." Strung along, one every rod, gulls were like "a fleet in line of battle."

Eagles, ospreys, bitterns, owls are stately naval ships of the line or revenue cutters or powerful steamers. Thoreau is amused by an owl pursued by a crow, "like a seventy-four among schooners."[7] His grandest salute, however, is to the fish hawk, or osprey, "aerial brother of the wave which he sails over and surveys." On March 31, 1842 he had a splendid view of one from a cliff. The majesty of its sailing kept returning to haunt him. "I cannot forget the majesty of that bird," he wrote three days later. "It was no sloop or smaller craft hove in sight, but a ship of the line, worthy to struggle with the elements." So it was that this great aerial performer, embodying the very "poetry of motion," earned an enviable notice four months later in Thoreau's essay-review, "The Natural History of Massachusetts," where the description is enlarged somewhat and ends with insistent stress on the nautical feeling it engendered. "Its [a stuffed specimen's] shrill scream seems yet to linger in its throat, the roar of the sea in its wings.... It reminds me of the Argonautic expedition."

The impression never faded. Nine years later Thoreau elevated the osprey to a symbolic role and shifted his vocabulary in accordance with a recent and famous international yachting event, the capture of the "America's cup" by the yacht *America* in August, 1851. Seen circling once again over a pine wood below him, it was "as if that hawk were made to be the symbol of my thought, how bravely he came round over those parts of the wood which he had not surveyed, taking in a new segment, annexing new territories! Without 'heave-yo!' it trims its sail. It goes about without the creaking of a block. The America yacht of the air never makes a tack, though it rounds the globe itself, takes in and shakes out its reefs without a flutter, its skyscrapers [sky topsails] all under its control.... If there are two concentrically circling, it is such a regatta as Southampton waters never witnessed." In 1859, moved by the flight of a marsh hawk, he elevated the bird to the highest pinnacle of all, the perfect symbol of perfect wildness and poetic genius.[8]

Here is part of Thoreau's elegy for a "youthful hawk, the proud bird of prey, the tenant of the skies," shot down by an irate farmer:

> We shall no more see his wave-like outline against a cloud, nor hear his scream from behind one.... Those wings which swept the sky must now dust the chimney-corner, perchance. So weaponed, with strong beak and talons, and wings, like a war-steamer, to carry them about. In vain were the brown-spotted eggs laid, in vain were ye cradled in the loftiest pine of the swamp.[9]

Most of the ships that Thoreau knew had their counterparts in the ocean of birds. Ducks and geese, so very native to the wetlands around Concord, were such excellent navigators both on the water and in the air that Thoreau seems to exhaust his vocabulary. Geese were splendid for the extent of their voyages, "not flitting from hedge to hedge, but from latitude to latitude, from State to State, steering boldly out into the ocean of air," like annual vessels announcing the season.[10] The image of the annual vessel arriving in Hudson Bay he often found useful in this connection, but the punctual spring arrival of all migrating birds he also thought "more sure than the arrival of [Atlantic] sailing and steam packets."

Ducks, especially mergansers and wood ducks, delighted him. They were at various times paddle-wheel steamers, revenue cutters, pirate craft, black schooners, or clippers. Early in the *Week* ducks "by the hundred, all uneasy in the surf" are described characteristically. They take off "with a clatter and a whistling, like riggers [square riggers] straight for Labrador, flying against the stiff gale with reefed wings."

Among the small birds Thoreau's attention seems to have been held principally by birdsong; yet whenever their flight was particularly noticeable they too navigated the aerial ocean. Goldfinches, in their long looping flight rising and falling seemed to him to skim "close over unseen billows," an action swifter but not unlike that of Canada geese "breasting the air and pushing it before them." Swallows are the fish of the air. The crow is not a good flyer against the wind, but "just like a vessel" must tack four or five times. An ascending flock explodes like a powder mill, but a flock of blackbirds is like a wave striking against a cliff "dashed upwards and lost in fine spray."

In these passages nautical figures mix with those from farming (a flying formation of geese like a harrow) and the military (sentinels and regimentals). The preponderance of the nautical, however, is nicely illustrated in the description of the American bittern or stake-driver. For Thoreau he is driving pilings. In flight he is a "long, ungainly craft, or revenue cutter, looking into harbors, and if it finds a fisherman there, standing out again." Seen in stormy weather, bitterns are "the mail of the seasons;" then they "lay to." Standing along the shore like sentries, they nevertheless coil their necks backward "as a sailor might a rope." When the bittern takes off, "it launches off," its breast in flight "a prominent cutwater."[11]

So much for the aerial sea, a skyscape in terms of a seascape. The Atlantic Ocean and its shore were different matters, infinitely more suggestive, grander in scope, and more pregnant with universal meanings. Environmentally ever near, modified by the daily activities of men, the seashore drew Thoreau like the proverbial magnet and provided him with a metaphor that ranks with some better known ones, the traveler and the ocean voyage for quest, or spring and dawn for renewal. Representative instances will establish its scope and variety of application and prepare us to move on to *Cape Cod*, a work wherein the dramatic image of mariner-terrener man standing on the lofty edge of the continent has a power and a meaning beyond its function as the end of the long walk from elbow to tip of the Cape.

The shore image is complicated by several dualities. The basic mariner-terrener duality offers two points of view: that of man living along the edge of the land and that of man sailing along the edge of the sea in coastal waters. There are in addition several points and degrees in middleness. From the picture of the mariner coasting along the shore, for example, came Thoreau's rather frequently used related image of the bold promontory, which I shall call "cape and headland." We have already seen that it is the outline of the scarlet oak leaf's edge that prepossessed Thoreau, with its cape and headlands. Cape headland viewed from the sea characteristically symbolized difficulties to be overcome, or some mystical goal that is to be reached by the navigating soul (or never to be reached) along the continuous shoreline of life. It is prominent in the *Week* whenever the waters spread out into broad bodies suggesting the size and mystery of the sea. Three of the book's four bits of dedicatory verse are primarily marine rather than fluvial and set the imaginative tone for the whole book. The first is the dedication to Thoreau's brother. The second announces that he is bound for "a distant shore," some "far Azore," seeking treasure. The third and longest prepares us for his many later postures as coastal mariner rather than inland *voyageur* or global navigator, following ocean shores of strange lands.

I sailed up a river with a pleasant wind,
New Lands, new people, and new thoughts to find;
Many fair reaches and headlands appeared,
And many dangers were there to be feared;
But when I remember where I have been
And the fair landscape that I have seen,
THOU seemst the only permanent shore,
The cape never rounded, nor wander'd o'er.[12]

The headland and the shore from the start were appropriate broad social symbols. As a young Harvard graduate and beginning school teacher, Thoreau did not hesitate to tackle grand themes. Stimulated by his reading of Goethe and impressed with Goethe's remark that whereas talent is built in solitude, character is made by living in "the stream of the world," he composed a lecture on "Society" and read it before the Concord Lyceum in April of 1838. In it he pleaded for a society made for men, not men for society. Seek the solid base of things, he said. "Let not society be the element in which you swim, or are tossed about at the mercy of the waves, but rather a strip of firm land running out into the sea, whose base is daily washed by the tide, but whose summit only the spring tide can reach." A year later, pondering the same question, he wrote, "There is a *terra firma* in society as well as geography, some whose ports you make by dead reckoning in all weather." The subject is the same in these two entries, obviously; but in the first the human figure is a landsman and in the second a mariner. They are not yet merged into mariner-terrener man. What should be observed is that from the time of his earliest speculations on the subject Thoreau pictured man standing on firm ground *in society*. Later on he was to insist on standing on the most seaward edge of that *terra firma* of life, where a profitable confrontation may take place. In *Passage to Walden* Reginald Cook wrote, "If [Thoreau's] nature mysticism signifies anything to us, it is that the visible world is but the threshold of an invisible one." Thoreau's word was more likely to be "shore."[13]

Mariner and terrener come together in the shore phenomenon of shipwreck, which provoked mixed feelings in him. At Cohasset he was presented with a veritable panorama of death. On the one hand he reacted with familiar transcendental hope that the victims may have been shipwrecked into some better or higher life. On the other hand he found himself coolly analytical, as the stark presence of so many corpses ("empty hulks") dulled his sense of tragedy. "It is the individual and the private that demands our sympathy." A single body on a lonely beach, he allows, would be more moving. Mass death is but the habit of nature. A man can really behold but one corpse, attend but one funeral.[14]

Wrecks and wrecked mariners on the shore, however, were also vivid reminders of nature's sublimity and power, even her bounty. Long before he came to regard the shore as the invaluable middle place, "the most advantageous point from which to contemplate this world," he had written in his *Journal* regarding woodsmen,

> When I contemplate a hard and bare life in the woods, I find my last consolation in its trivialness. Shipwreck is less distressing because the breakers do not trifle with us. . . . The dripping mariner finds consolation and sympathy in the infinite sublimity of the storm. With courage he can lay down his life on the strand, for it never turned a deaf ear to him, nor had he ever exhausted its sympathy.[15]

Here the mariner merely illustrates the woodsman. Land and sea are thrown together, however, in equal balance in a powerful statement in the Spring section of *Walden*. Whereas shipwreck is the first of four instances of the violence that betrays the inexhaustible vigor and sublimity of nature, the language of the passage focuses attention on a close land-and-sea parallel.

> At the same time that we are earnest to explore and learn all things, we require that all things be mysterious and unexplorable, that land and sea be infinitely wild, unsurveyed, and unfathomed by us because unfathomable. We can never have enough of nature. We must be refreshed by the sight of inexhaustible vigor, vast and titantic features, the sea-coast with its wrecks, the wilderness with living and decaying, the thunder-clouds, and the rain which lasts three weeks and produces freshets.

The mariner-terrener remark in his review of Etzler's book comes in between these two passages, suggesting that land-sea parallels, involving man both fortunate and unfortunate on the shore, were settling into dependable analogies.

Thoreau's descriptions of shipwreck derive from experience with the fact at Staten Island, Fire Island, Cohasset, and Cape Cod, at all of which places he saw wrecks, wreckage, corpses of victims, and professional wreckers. One shipwreck which scattered a cargo of rags, juniper berries, and bitter almonds furnished him with a graphic example in *Life Without Principle* of the triviality of most commerce. His fascination with wreckage and with the daily occupation of professional salvagers ("wreckers") along the beach at Cape Cod is evidenced by the extraordinary amount of space he allotted to the subject. The unselfconscious union of man with the elements is caught when he notes that the "bleached and weatherbeaten face" of one old wrecker seemed like an old sail. Wrecks and wreckage of course meant the simple realistic fact of suffering and loss, but there were also gains. This was the first thing that the ocean had to say to him there. "But are we not all wreckers," he wrote, "contriving that some treasure be washed up on our beach...? The sea, vast and wild as it is, bears thus the waste and wrecks of human art to its remotest shores." He also saw that "the beauty of the shore was wrecked for many a lonely walker there, until he could perceive at last, how its beauty was enhanced by wrecks like this, and acquired a rarer and sublimer beauty still."[16]

Some deep emotional experiences, furthermore, were inextricably associated with the seashore. There was his youthful visit to Scituate in company with his brother John to see Ellen Sewall with whom both boys were in love, and with whom they walked the beach in a common state of emotional ecstasy. Both were ultimately rejected by the docile young lady who bowed to absolute parental authority. There was for Henry David the later visit with Joseph Osgood, the man whom Ellen did marry. The two men, the successful and the rejected lover, took a long walk on the beach at Cohasset where they talked and viewed the wreck of the *St. John*. There was his journey to Fire Island to identify and recover if possible the body of Margaret Fuller Ossoli, friend, critic, and fellow transcendentalist. A gruesome task. And in the same year there was the discovery at Cape Cod that the sea was completely indifferent to man. It was not for Thoreau to luxuriate very much at the shore; his mind and feelings were too intensely engaged.

It was on the beach at Scituate that Thoreau began to compose his little poetic *apologia*, the poem "The Fisher's Son," which Carl Bode feels is his fullest characterization of his way of life.[17] Elsewhere Thoreau wrote that he had thought "the sun of our love should have risen as noiselessly as the sun out of the sea, and we sailors have found ourselves steering between the tropics as if the broad day had lasted forever."[18] But the sun did not rise, and four months after his great disappointment he entered in his *Journal*, "How alone our life must be lived! We dwell on the seashore, and none between us and the sea." This was part of the "calendar of the ebbs and flows of the soul," about which he had already soliloquized concerning his *Journal*: "Let the daily tide leave some deposit on these pages, as it leaves sand and shells on the shore. So much increase of *terra firma*. . .as on these sheets as a beach, the waves may cast up pearls and seaweed." In the essay, *Walking*, created from jottings in the early 1850's, the edge-of-the-world, ebb-and-flow of things is restated. "I live a sort of border life, on the confines of a world into which I make occasional and transient forays only."[19]

Probably the most intense expression of Thoreau's need for solitude and his yearning for spiritual affinities is concentrated in the four stanzas of "The Fisher's Son" which he printed in the *Week*. The symbolism of the middle place is magnified by being doubled. Besides the tide-washed beach as a locus, he introduces a middle deep or sea, which is coastal water. In this design an edge of the sea meets the edge of the land.

My life is like a stroll upon the beach,
As near the ocean's edge as I can go;
My tardy steps its waves sometimes o'erreach,
Sometimes I stay to let them overflow.

My sole employment 't is, and scrupulous care,
To place my gains beyond the reach of tides,
Each smoother pebble, and each shell more rare,
Which ocean kindly to my hand confides.

I have but few companions on the shore,
They scorn the strand who sail upon the sea,
Yet oft I think the ocean they've sailed o'er
Is deeper known upon the strand to me.

The middle sea contains no crimson dulse,
Its deeper waves cast up no pearls to view,
Along the shore my hand is on its pulse,
And I converse with many a shipwrecked crew.[20]

When in love, Thoreau had briefly sailed this sea. Washed ashore after his rejection, he entered in his *Journal* a despairing passage that seems to be the immediate germ of this poem. "I am stranded at each reflux of the tide—I who sailed as boyantly [sic] on the middle deep as a ship am as helpless as a muscle [sic] on a rock."[21] There are two other longer versions of the poem, and there is evidence in Thoreau's manuscripts of much revision, indicating some continuing concern.

Using the shore thus to symbolize man's engagement with the two major elements in his fate, matter and spirit, Thoreau is careful to sustain the functions of both. Total involvement in either is not desirable. In the sea of spirit he enjoys only short forays, brief voyages, or periodic overflows. Unlike true religious mystics, who strive for union with God in a world of pure spirit, Thoreau keeps his feet on the ground, his head in air of now. Soft yearnings for escape into the realm of spirit (immortality) is unacceptable to this thoughtful man. Thus in the Sunday section of the *Week* he rejects Christian hope. The middle, the *terra firma* of his many shore figures, is here daringly reaffirmed. Christ "taught man but imperfectly how to live; his thoughts were all directed toward another world. There is another kind of success than this. Even here we have another sort of living to get, and must buffet it somehow longer. There are various tough problems yet to solve, and we must make shift to live, betwixt spirit and matter, such a life as we can." It is his challenge to those men who have "a singular desire to be good without being good for anything." This vitalism, reminiscent of William Blake, is restated somewhat later in his *Journal*, "We do not commonly live our life out and full; we do not inspire and expire fully and freely and entirely enough, so that the wave, the comber, of each inspiration shall break upon our extremest shores, rolling till it meets the sand which bounds us. . . ."[22]

No doubt this accounts in part for his detestation of languid summer crowds at newly popular seaside resorts like Newport. The fashionable "going to the beach" suggested to him only "failure and defeat." City people "succumb and slope to the beach for six weeks" for the kind of therapy and antidote Emerson pictures in his verse dialogue, *Seashore*. Maiden ladies with servants and medicine bottles "energetically keep cool," cries Thoreau, tossing the whole thing aside like an old bottle and calling for a journey to the beach "after another fashion." That fashion is not revealed in the *Journal* passage in which these invectives appear. A day later, however, in the kind of echo we get accustomed to in extended reading of the *Journal*, he makes it delightfully clear in a comment on young swallows being taken by the parent birds to perch on the telegraph wires where the parents teach them to fly. Thoreau ends cryptically, "They have gone to their beach." Their beach, the true beach, is the opposite of a sanatorium; it is a place of larger activity where may be found new experience, learning, maturity, power, and productivity.[23]

One of the "tough problems" that Thoreau faced was isolation. Contrary to popular misconception, though he loved solitude and resisted intrusion on his zealously guarded privacy, he nevertheless yearned for kindred souls with whom to share and exchange experience and from whom to receive support and confirmation and joy. He never found that soul, though his brother John, companion on the Concord and Merrimac rivers, Ellen Sewall of Scituate, and the Emersons seemed the likeliest candidates. Under differing circumstances all were cut out of or faded from his life and Thoreau seems never to have come close to any one thereafter.

Thus it is that he wrote so much about Friendship. The word as he used it was a covering term for a close, hopefully ideal, human relationship where kindred spirits regardless of sex not only were attracted to one another, but were capable of a working union. It encompassed what is ordinarily called friendship, but also companionship, kinship, fraternal love, and love between the sexes. Some critics have seen in Thoreau's concept a screen for the expression of his frustrated love for Ellen Sewall and Lidian Emerson, and for homosexual tendencies, but the subject is much larger than this. Friendship is an ideal union but not a static nor sapless one. Thoeau is careful to insist it is an energizing state and must possess "the principle of growth." It does not cut him off from "the large and respectable nation of Acquaintances," those everyday people ("Strangers and Enemies") with whom he declares he can live in a certain mutual usefulness.

Friendship is the subject of the longest essay in the *Week*, from which the phrases above have been taken. It is the subject of many of his poems. It appears frequently in the early years of his *Journal*, and through it we are able to recognize the pain he suffered in his changing relationshp with the Emersons. It was therefore a matter of great importance, and his failures in the matter pose some thorny questions which it is not necessary here to pursue. What is of interest in the present discussion is that this deeply and hopelessly idealized relationship, in which he is constantly aware of his failures, he presented in many nautical metaphors: of sailing, of infinite seas, and of ships and capes and shores. "In the love of narrow souls I make many short voyages, but in vain; I find no sea-room. But in the great souls I sail before the wind without a watch, and never reach the shore." The evidence is plentiful that he never achieved the exaltation of the latter ideal state. He always returned to or was washed ashore.

More characteristically Thoreau pictures the miracle of friendship taking place on an island or the shore. If an island, the important topographical part was the shore. In the *Journal* for January 29, 1840, he wrote, "The nearest approach to a community of love these days is like the distant breaking of waves on the seashore. An ocean there must be, for it washes our beach. This alone do all men sail for, trade for, plow for, preach for, fight for." This is prepared for by remarks describing friendship as evanescent, fair and flitting like a summer cloud, magical. The friend "is some fair floating isle of palms eluding the mariner in Pacific seas." There are many dangers, but "who would not sail through mutiny and storm...to reach the fabulous retreating shores of some continent man?" The two poems, "The Atlantides" and "Sea and Land but his Neighbors" (elsewhere called "The Friend"), balance one another in that the first deals with the far away and the second deals with the local and familiar. "The Atlantides" speaks of "fabled shores" that none ever reaches, though dotted outlines of "our main" are still found on the oldest charts. In this poem no mariner ever finds "our beach," and the Friend is islanded in "an Atlantic mystery." In "Sea and Land..." the Friend's position is more recognizable, but the metaphysical conceits must be read carefully. The Friend sits alone on the strand gazing toward the sea looking for marine news. "Many men dwell far inland, / But he alone sits on the strand" always gazing seaward. Friendship in the figure is wholly a marine matter. "Marine news he ever reads," and at every word a landsman speaks and in "every companion's eye / A sailing vessel doth descry." He furthermore hears in ocean's sullen roar news of broken friendships, distant wrecks and ventures of past years. Four prose sentences later comes the cryptic remark, "There goes a rumor that the earth is inhabited, but the shipwrecked mariner has not seen a footprint on the shore." The gaunt message therefore is: It is commonly thought that the world is full of real and potential friends, but the spiritually sensitive man seeking a true Friend sees no sign of any. He feels his isolation, and he dwells on the middle ground between the practical and the ideal. This is the way things are.

In the forty lines of a longer, topheavy version of "The Friend," which Carl Bode prints,[24] we see Thoreau struggling to enlarge the theme of mariner-terrener man, shore-dwelling and forever gazing expectantly seaward, into a speculation of what would happen if the landsman friend ever found a sailor friend and a spiritual East Indiaman (their union) were ever to appear in normal ship channels bringing the riches of the East in her hold. It would put an end to ordinary commerce, and men would

> ...sail the sea no more,
> The sea itself become a shore
> To a broader, deeper sea,
> A profounder mystery.

The failure of the dream only points up Thoreau's ultimate stoical realism. He accepts his beach, with its burden of unfulfillment. In the spirit of consciously working at one of the tough problems yet to solve, he turned four months after the publication of the *Week* to an examination of the Atlantic Ocean at Cape Cod. At once he was faced with violence, death, and titanic nonhuman power. It was his second experience of this kind, though less shattering than his discovery atop Mt. Katahdin two years before that raw nature is not a possible habitation for man. At Cape Cod he saw a more understandable, though not always comfortable, face of nature. The incessantly rolling sea was "too far-traveled and untamable to be familiar." The sea's positive values as a womb of life (we are all "products of the sea-slime") were balanced by the sobering concept of the sea as a "vast morgue." It was "naked nature," superhuman, "wasting no thought on man, nibbling at the cliffy shores." Its immensity "was awful to consider, and it appeared to have no relation to the friendly land, either as shore or bottom.... I felt I was a land animal." This somewhat terrifying experience remained forever linked with the image of the "neutral" seashore, as we find when Thoreau later sat on Mt. Monadnock (June, 1858). "It often reminded me of my walks on the beach, and suggested how much both depend for their sublimity on solitude and dreariness. In both cases we feel the presence of some vast, titanic power." In the grip of this power he saw himself, saw man that is, as a shore dweller identified with a middle stage in the evolutionary process, struggling to see "what proportion man and his works bear to the globe." Though he allows in *Cape Cod* that "the Ocean is the origin of all things," it is more pertinent to view it as "the laboratory of continents;" for land animals and plants, he deduced, are higher "in the scale of being" than marine forms, on their "way to the heavens."[25]

Thoreau's *Cape Cod* is far more than a book about the sea. "I went to see the seashore," he said. It evokes the genius of a place. It is a loosely arranged, easy-going digest of three rambles along the beach, with some criss-crossing of the Cape itself. The casual pace combined with frequent lightness of tone earned for it at one time a reputation as popular journalism. Thoreau himself was embarrassed by the spontaneous laughter of audiences when he presented episodes in lyceum lectures.

People got the humor but missed the point. Today *Cape Cod* is cited as a kind of other *Walden*, the record of an earnest spiritual quest. The long account does cohere, and beneath an often playful exterior it reveals basic Thoreauvian ideas. On the beach and the bank, where man is stripped, his "works are wrecks." He must (at least he can try to) come to terms with himself in the face of elemental life-forces. It is a picture of the profitable discovery of an unspoiled American scene where the sea (real and symbolic) meets the land, and where the effects of such a meeting on both the Cape folk and the peripatetic witty philosopher deserve the closest attention. The persistent pairing of sea and land, furthermore, sets up an antiphonal rhetorical mode that gives the work organic structure.

American sea captains and fishermen traditionally lived in two worlds: the autocratic community of the ship and the democratic community of their seacoast towns. In the resident folk of the Cape, Thoreau found an example of a complete and homogeneous people on whom nature (the sea) had set her stamp—a simple, genuine, relatively unspoiled people who had no need to simplify, because they were already simple. They did not have to seek nature, because they were nature's offspring perfectly adapted to their environment. The Cape Cod boy was a sailor by the time he could walk. "He leaps from his leading strings into the shrouds, it is but a bound from the mother's lap to the masthead. He boxes the compass in his infant soliloquies. He can hand, reef, and steer by the time he flies a kite."[26]

Thoreau is explicit that the point of viewing is the land. His "book on Cape Cod" opens with the simple statement that he went there three times "to get a better view" of the ocean than he had yet had. Then lest the readers assume this meant he was about to present an exhaustive study of the sea, which would mean turning sailor for at least a time, he sets them right in the sentence that follows. In the spirit and language of his mariner-terrener review he warns, "but having come so fresh to the sea, I have got but little salted. My readers must expect only so much saltness as the land breeze acquires from blowing over an arm of the sea, or is tasted on the windows and the barks of trees twenty miles inland, after September gales." An inland man, he has latterly "extended [his] excursions to the seashore." And finally, lest "excursions to the seashore" be still short of the mark, he opens his second paragraph with, "I did not see why I might not make a book on Cape Cod, as well as my neighbor on 'Human Culture.' It is but another name for the same thing." His scope is to be broad. He will view ocean, beach, dune, and backyard, since, as he wrote later, "All nature is to be regarded as it concerns man."[27]

His engaging vignettes of people and towns never stand alone. There is always the felt presence of the sea, its sounds, its weather moods, its fitful bounty. This merging of sea and land in a total community is the important thing. In the fact that it is the merging of global waters with the edge of America, it is the theme of the book.

Thus he ranged and talked with Cape Cod men of all ages and indulged his gift for conviviality and humor as never before. His account of the old Wellfleet oysterman needs no special mention. He wished he could stay all winter and sit about and tell stories. Sailors' yarns he thought were not only entertaining but significant, though science ignored them. These seafaring folk, like those of Nantucket, were the very audience for him. And his book was destined to be the kind of "villageous" book he recommended to his friend Ricketson as appropriate for Ricketson's history of New Bedford.

Many moods and colors and actions of the sea along the shore he managed to experience and describe: the fearful storms and brutal destruction, the transparent water and the transparent October air, the sludgy shallows full of seaweed, kelp, and jellyfish, the yield of mackerel and cod to the picturesque fleets of schooners offshore and away at the Banks. The scenes for the most part are on a grand scale—raw, vibrant, and ever-changing yet enduring, plentifully supplied with lonely waste places necessary, he says, for getting the feel of things—the wild. It all seemed so indigenous that he admittedly over-indulged his habit of making notes on local history, "extracts" from gazettes, histories, and accounts of explorations. In his last two chapters he indulges in two extravagant whimsies that we neglect at some risk. The first is the amusing shouted conversation with Europe from the beach above the Highland Light on the last day of his tour. This is surely the loudest and most distantly projected dialogue before the electronic era. After conventional musing about gazing east from our shores straight over to Portugal, he shouts his boisterous American brag. His mind's eye travels north along the Portuguese shore until he sights Cape Finisterre at the southern tip of the Bay of Biscay. Land's End? What a "vain brag." "Here is Cape Cod,—Cape Land's-Beginning," he shouts back. Then letting his eye swing south to the Straits of Gibraltar, the Pillars of Hercules, he asks Europe what is written on them. "The inhabitants shouted *Ne plus ultra* (no more beyond), but the wind bore to us the truth only, *plus ultra* (more beyond), and over the Bay westward was echoed *ultra* (beyond)." And finally in his excitement he enlarges the meaning of the Cape as Land's Beginning to include the whole American continent, advising Europeans to pull up stakes and come west even to the shores of California, "the only *plus ultra* now." Satisfied that he had "taken the wind out of their sails," he moves on to the wrist of the Cape.

He is now near the end. But instead of picking up speed, he indulges in a long (thirty-page) historical aside, an "Ante-Pilgrim history of New

England." A modern editor relegates this to small print in an appendix, if he bothers with it at all. But it is curiously germane, revealing Thoreau's persistent need for getting the sense of places and his feeling for New England in particular as durable seashore. Says he: came the Norsemen, came the superb French explorers and mapmakers, the great Italian navigators, the trading and colonizing Dutch and English, yet the shore endured as it always had. Cape Cod was still the Cape of codfish and white sands. Discovered and rediscovered, named and renamed, it was always "even then Cape and Bay." It was an object lesson in the permanence of nature as against the ephemeral character of men and nations. It did not need a past or a present. It *was*. It was profoundly American and thus significant in the history of human culture. The sea shaped and was shaping not only its shores but its destiny. Cape Cod was significant.

Cape Cod ends dramatically, though not where we expect it to, in Boston harbor as the little yacht *Olata* nudges into her berth bringing Thoreau home. Five more pages add a kind of coda disguised as a traveler's guide. This recapitulates intended meanings in the book and makes sure the reader's attention is brought back to the tip of the Cape. These are the highlights he wants remembered: He went to view and confront the ocean. There is not another beach on the Atlantic coast like Cape Cod where there is a double way, "a beach and a bank, which at the same time shows you the land and the sea." It is the "edge of the continent;" others are mere sandbars. Wellfleet is most attractive because "it best combines the country and the seaside." Fall is the best season to go, for "then the atmosphere is more transparent" and provides "scope for eye and mind." It is unknown to the fashionable world, which is more interested in bowling, circular railroads, and wine than brine. It is necessary to see the death-dealing storms of autumn and winter "in order to get the impression that the sea is calculated to make." The coda then narrows down to four pungent sentences which tellingly re-recapitulate the whole, driving home selected themes: "Here is the spring of springs, the waterfall of waterfalls" (the Grand Source). "A storm. . . is the time to visit it" (Unleashed Power). "A lighthouse or a fisherman's hut [is] the true hotel" (Noble Simplicity of Shore people). "A man may stand there and put all America behind him" (the Perfect Place for Man, between this Land and the Sea).

The last sentence is seductively simple and has caused some puzzlement.[28] Yet it is logical and functional as well as teasingly climactic. We should note that it is a general impersonal statement. Not *I* or *We* stand *here*, but *a man* may stand *there*. How universal does Thoreau intend this man to be? Any man? An American? A man like himself? Keeping in mind Thoreau's repeated assertion that the proper habitation for man is on a seashore (between the solid earth of reality and the great tidal flow of infinite spiritual power), that man is a land animal, but that he should be a mariner-terrener exposing himself to the influences of the sea, we have first of all to identify this Cape-standing man with the Thoreauvian idealization. Also, he says *there*, pointing *to* his figure and suggesting some special recognition of an understood character of Cape Cod.

As the super-Thoreau stands there feeling kinship with honest fishermen and lightkeepers, and putting all America at his back, he gazes eastward toward old Europe. He has not rejected America nor turned his back on it; he is backed up to its solidness. He is deliberately, dynamically positioning himself, a part of that historically rich land-mass—a kind of American Colossus larger than life and emblematic of Thoreau's whole experience in expanded consciousness on Cape Cod. He is merged with sea, air, land, and history. The place is not just a place where "the lesson and impression of the sea" may sink deep; it is the representative place in Thoreau, the seashore of seashores where the exterior and interior life may mingle, a second Walden well rooted and strongly backed, fronting a universe of fearful symmetry, power, and promise.

Inasmuch as man can expect at best brief journeys into the marine depths of his nature or into the mysteries of the habitable universe, the best life is lived along a symbolic shore where he can either be revitalized or destroyed, or both, "for always the same strain which is a dirge to one household is a morning song of rejoicing to another." Usually the man of searching spirit is revitalized. He may not get answers to his questions, but he is afforded poignant awareness of a greater than he. Being on the shore, *this* shore as he reminds Longfellow while amending a line in Longfellow's poem "Seaweed," he is in a position to hear the sea's "pure and unqualified strain of eternal melody" and to discover new unrecorded "grotesque and fabulous thoughts" symbolized by drifting seaweed.[29] This is the right way "to take Cape Cod," he reminds his friend Harrison Blake in a letter scolding Blake for not having "persevered in walking on the beach and on the bank, even to land's end."[30]

Thoreau sometimes pictures the human figure on his seashore, thus, as relatively passive, hoping for seventh waves and tides that bring ashore the hoped-for reassurance of spiritual power. More often, however, the seeker is vibrant and active, probing for meaning, knocking at the gate, the strings of his being responding like "the lyre, which ever lies on the shore," whether he sits beside Walden Pond or stands on Cape Cod. In both he is struggling to get down to essentials. His vision is stoic in the pristine sense of perceiving the universe as one divine entity and learning to accept it without delusion. In this he is positive and personal, never reaching the poignant pitch of Ishmael's cry about the sea: "It is the image of the ungraspable phantom of life; and this is the key to it all." Thoreau's sea flashed symbols of imagination and spirit, tokens of infinity occasionally touching human life, but offering a vision of possibility rather than an ungraspable phantom.

Looking back now, we are perhaps not surprised to find that Thoreau's first extended maritime figure concerns Zeno, who "stood in precisely the same relation to the world that I do Now. He is forsooth, bred a merchant...and can trade and barter, and perchance higgle, and moreover he can be shipwrecked and cast ashore at the Piraeus, like one of your Johns or Thomases. He strolls into a shop and is charmed by a book by Xenophon—and straightway becomes a philosopher. The sun of a new life's day rises to him,—serene and unclouded,—which looks over *stoa*. And still the fleshly Zeno sails on, shipwrecked, buffeted, tempest-tossed; but the true Zeno sails even a placid sea." Seven days later he entered the note already alluded to. The true student recognizes "no Past, no Present; but wherever he emerges from the bosom of time, his course is not with the sun,...but ever toward the seashore."[31]

On the Deck of the World

If your trade is with the Celestial Empire, then some small counting house on the coast, in some Salem harbor, will be fixture enough.... I have thought that Walden Pond would be a good place for business...it is a good port and a good foundation.

Walden

The Style and gentility of a ship and her crew depend upon the length and character of the voyage. An India or China voyage always is *the thing,* and a voyage to the Northwest coast...for furs is romantic and mysterious, and if it takes a ship round the world, by way of the Islands and China, it outranks them all.

Dana, *Two Years Before the Mast*

I was surprised by the sound of my own voice. It is an atmosphere burdened with thought....My life had been a River Platte, tinkling over its sands but useless for all great navigation, but now it suddenly became a fathomless ocean. It shelved off to unimagined depths.

Journal

VI

On the Deck of the World

THE COURSE TOWARD THOREAU'S SEASHORE was "great navigation," an epic act. In great navigation the mariner searches for more than a proper home for man; he sails toward "some continent man" himself. And as the contemplation of man begins at home, the search was for Thoreau's own deepest self. Thus it is that the important function of Winter, solitary thinking, is celebrated through this metaphor. *Walden* is shaped by it. It is the vital *modus operandi* of the *Week*. It is the structural center of "Autumnal Tints." It is the great quotable paragraph in "Life Without Principle." And many lesser places in Thoreau's writings reveal the relevance and usefulness of it, as he persists in reaffirming his most meaningful concept; the importance of mental life and the search for inner realities.

On August 31, 1856 Thoreau was annoyed. As he was about to embark on the river, some quite unacceptable "heavy fellow" waylaid him and asked if he could go along. Thoreau's annoyance streams out over two pages of vivid warning in his *Journal* of just what he was about when he voyaged on the Concord. "There sits one by the shore," he begins, who is not aware that if he takes him in his boat, he must take him into his mind as well. Nothing Thoreau ever wrote states as explicitly that his purpose was to live a free and unconfined *mental* life. With this man along, his mind "would surely founder in such a voyage as I was contemplating. I know very well that I should never reach that expansion of the river I have in mind, with him aboard with his terrene qualities. He would sink my bark (not to another sea) and never know it." Thoreau could better load his boat with mud and sit on the tholepins; he would at least have room and "could reach that expansion of the river" nevertheless. He "must be fancy free."

There follows a playful paragraph starting with the paradox: "If you could go without going, then you might go." The dull fellow says he "could go in the steerage," but Captain Thoreau says, no, no; you would dump your luggage there, then settle yourself right down in the captain's stateroom. Your baggage? Yes. Yourself? "Anything, my dear sir, but yourself."

This very revealing passage ends with the familiar fiction of himself as sea trader with clearly defined responsibilities. "This company is obliged to make a distinction between dead freight and passengers. . . . The good ship sails when she is ready. For freight or passengers apply to——?? Ask my friend where."

These remarks are a typical exhibition of Thoreau's imaginative involvement with the grander aspect of sailing, the ocean voyage. The deep-water navigator who pilots a large vessel, and who is engaged in a long, responsible, and difficult voyage, provided all the elements of the heroic: Thoreau's vital and recurring deep-water images are both explicit and implicit, a momentary simile perhaps for description or a metaphor of almost mythic power.

Thoreau may stand on Mt. Wachusett or Mt. Monadnock observing afar off the morning fog creating islands out of other promontories, and feel that he was standing on the deck of a ship in the South Pacific, "the earth itself. . . like a blue Pacific island, where who knows what islanders inhabit? and as we sail near its shores, we see the waving of the trees and hear the lowing of the kine."[1] Or at Cape Cod, "standing on that narrow Cape" was like "being on the deck of a vessel. . . thirty miles at sea." There is his picture in another place in *Cape Cod* of the Cape seen from the packet that was taking him back to Boston. In the distance it seemed like a great ship "hull down" on the horizon. These are slight and merely descriptive. On the other hand, his image of standing "on the deck of the world" in the Conclusion of *Walden* is a powerful expression of his life at a moment of climax. The range and power in Thoreau of this one figure have been diminished by those commentators who see it merely as a conventional literary metaphor.

When Thoreau, camping in some Merrimac snug harbor, writes that there he could read "the journal of some other sailor, whose bark had ploughed, perchance, more famous and classic seas," he is suggesting that the long boat trip on the placid New England streams itself might also perchance be in its way classic and famous, that it might not be so foolishly extravagant as his pseudo-nautical language sounded—in fact, that it should be understood as a voyage over great mental depths.

He gives us fair warning that this is to be so even before he starts down the Concord River. Sherman Paul, I believe, is the only writer on Thoreau who has seen the real significance of the first chapter, called "Concord River." Yet a remark of that astute critic minimizes too much, it seems to me, the final significance of the sea voyage. Professor Paul calls the *Week* a prelude to *Walden*. Setting aside Emerson's impercipient comment that the *Week* "was a very slender thread for such big beads and ingots as are strung on it," Paul affirms its unity on both literal and spiritual levels, "a song of himself," the central theme being "the problem of inspiration, the organic life, and the quest for being." The structural metaphor, he finds, is "sailing by and into thought," an exploratory journey. The introductory chapter establishes the book's dimensions "by describing the perfect adaptation of his boat to the elements" wherein Thoreau gave us the hint that the book was to be concerned with "a soul's voyage," through the useful "enterprise of going to sea." Both river and sea were the brink of the unknown, and at the time of writing the *Week* they were wholly beneficent. These remarks are the most perceptive defining to date of the controlling figure for the book, and of what Thoreau is probing and searching for in his drifting sort of way. But they can be strengthened by further examination of Thoreau's feeling for the river and for the sea.

The river and the sea, Paul writes, stepping outside the *Week* for the moment, cannot be equated as symbols of the beneficence of nature because Thoreau later felt at Cape Cod the terrifying "otherness" of the sea, its "primordial nature apart from the interests of man." This I find to be not the whole story. And when Paul goes on to say, "He was never able to make the sea, as he was the river, the symbol of his profoundest needs and experiences,"[2] I find it necessary, in the light of Thoreau's heavy reliance upon sea and voyage symbols, to adjust the emphasis considerably.

A fruitful aspect of Thoreau's art is obscured if we try to distinguish so sharply between Thoreau's river symbolism and his symbolism of the sea. For the fact is that Thoreau merges the two in varying ways. In the Wednesday section of the *Week,* as we have already noted, he wrote, "The smallest stream is *mediterranean* sea, a smaller ocean creek within the land."[3] His own italics are not lost upon us, for in this merging the sea maintains its familiar and dominating symbolic position as a source of man's spiritual power. It is the uncharted element providing imaginable routes for inner guests and travels. And it is, along with stellar space, a goal of spiritual seeking. Streams in Thoreau, we should be reminded, not only run to the sea, an inevitable returning home, but they are also (even the sluggish Concord, as we have seen) forced upon our attention as estuaries of the sea. Walden Pond, too, in its capacity to stir the depths of human fancy was an ocean; and at Cape Cod he once remarked that the ocean was "but a larger lake." Gazing at the ocean from Staten Island, he doubted that he could lose Walden completely in it. Emerson fixed this idea of the non-existence of size quite acceptably for us in his famous funeral address: "To him there was no such thing as size. The pond was a small ocean; the Atlantic, a large Walden Pond."

Thoreau's most impressive celebration of rivers is the eloquent passage stimulated by a broad reach of the Merrimac, in the *Journal* for July 2, 1858. It begins with the revelation that such rivers liberate him from "the more terrene earth." His thoughts are "expanded and elevated." Such a winding river is "a highway to other continents" and "allies [him] to all the world." He found something equivalent to culture and civilization in it. "Its channel conducts our thoughts as well as our bodies to classic and famous ports."

There is no gainsaying that the river was a catalyst of the greatest importance to Thoreau. We should not forget, however, that this was so because his "eye and thoughts" were led "down its channel to the sea." It is thus superior "in its liberating influence" to a static lake. Thus it is, he ends, that "river towns are winged towns," which can be wafted by their rivers "over the world." The high purpose of rivers, then, is to link up with the great parent, the ocean stream, which from his very first meditation on the subject twenty years before, he knew was "the end of the matter." Indeed, in the *Week* he specifically rejects the fluency of the one-way-flowing river in favor of the more massive ebb and flow of ocean tides as a figure for thought and a style appropriate to its expression. "The flow of thought is more like a tidal wave than a river."[4]

Thoreau, furthermore, habitually pictures himself as an ocean voyager in and around Concord. One of his more famous paradoxes is, "I have travelled a good deal in Concord," an idea he first toyed with somewhere between 1845 and 1847 when he was putting together the *Week,* though the sentences finally lodged in *Walden.* For years it amused him. "It takes a genius to travel in his own country," he wrote on August 6, 1851, "to make any progress between his door and his gate. But such a traveller will make the distances which Hanno and Marco Polo and Cook and Ledyard[5] went over ridiculous."

As late as 1860 Thoreau was writing, "As I sailed the unexplored sea of Concord, many a dell and swamp and wooded hill is my Ceram and Amboyna." It is a long passage which repeats and intensifies his feeling that discovering the imaginative significance of the near and the ordinary is only another kind of voyage. He felt related to his native fields "as the navigator to undiscovered islands in the sea." Having walked over to Sudbury on a brilliant November day, he set down, "We journeyed into the foreign land of Sudbury to see how the Sudbury men. . . live."[6] This is how he "travelled a good deal in Concord."

Both the *Week* and *Walden* are cast in this mold. The *Week* opens with "Concord River," which is not so much an introduction as a prelude, having little to do directly with the narrative that follows, but which sets the tone of the work and reveals the mode and method of thought. The reader is warned that two strains make the book: the surface (river and landscape) and whatever lies beneath (thought, spirit, feeling). The way may be random and uncharted. The very digressions in the narrative, those "snags" which James Russell Lowell complained of, will be important explorations—unexpected, unpredictable, and unrelated only as the new islands, new coasts, and new continents encountered by the hazard-beset ocean explorer are.

The mood is created at once. The third group of couplets among the dedicatory verses facing page one have already given ample warning that a thoroughly Thoreauvian journey is intended. In this mood Thoreau then takes up a celebration of the majestic little Concord, which in antiquity and fame is equated with the Nile and the Euphrates, "a poet's stream" like Xanthus and Scamander, a stream "of personal importance in the annals of the world" like the Mississippi and the Ganges and the Nile once again. In the second paragraph of the chapter he proposes that "it is worth the while to make a voyage up this stream." And almost at once he is celebrating not merely the shallow grassy river, but Imagination that floats, as he is to say in the Sunday section, on the "more than Atlantic depth, and no danger of running aground." Travel *up* the river, says Thoreau, and you will meet whole new worlds of wild creatures and Homeric men. "You shall perhaps run aground on Cranberry Island...and get as good a freezing there as anywhere on the Northwest Coast. I never voyaged so far in all my life." This is how to sail on the Concord. It announces a voyage of mental exploration *down* the Concord and *up* the Merrimac where distant "Labradors" and "Northwest Passages" may be discovered. One can voyage far in Concord, and one can voyage far on the "ocean stream" of this book.

This is why the *Week* may be regarded as a trial run for *Walden.* On river or pond, the quest is inner and mental. The vital quality is a fluid if not always a fluvial movement, a process of flowing, sailing, drifting, pressing on under full sail into the unknown where "our own interior is white on the chart." So often does the symbolic ocean voyage appear in Thoreau's writings that it suggests a narrowing of the generic word "traveller" (his frequent synonym for man) to something like "navigator" whenever he intends mental and spiritual traveling. And as we shall see, he often lavished on this nautical metaphor plenty of accurate, circumstantial, concrete nautical details absorbed from his reading and his day-to-day familiarity with New England maritime affairs, so that such an exhortation as "explore the private sea" is pulled away from formal, virtually abstract statement to the concrete and active. The use of the voyage metaphor was almost a habit of mind, and through it we are invited to confront many of the solid centers of his thought and observe how well his meaning is vivified.

Three days after he moved into his hut at Walden Pond, his head full of Homeric intimations destined for both the *Week on the Concord and Merrimack Rivers* and *Walden,* he fleetingly identified himself with Ulysses, the greatest of all voyagers. "Fellow-wanderer and survivor,"

Thoreau sat "on the shore of [his own] Ithaca" and felt himself thrust forward into a life of thought, strongly aware that he was a descendant of a heroic tradition.[7] And the concept of himself as voyager in strange seas holds throughout *Walden.* It is prominent at the beginning and the end, and it comes mindfully to the surface at a number of places in between. Indeed, it provides a kind of contextual thread for the book.

As Thoreau revised his manuscript he made two interesting additions to the second and third paragraphs.[8] Near the end of the second he inserted the familiar sentence:

> Moreover, I, on my side, require of every writer, first or last, a simple and sincere account of his own life...some such account as he would send to his kindred from a distant land; for if he has lived sincerely, it must have been a distant land to me.

Then he proceeded to add a new long sentence to the opening of paragraph three:

> I would fain say something, not so much concerning the Chinese and Sandwich Islanders as you who read these pages, who are said to live in New England; something about your condition or circumstances in this world, in this town, what it is, whether it cannot be improved as well as not.

This prepares the reader for the famous paradox, "I have travelled a good deal in Concord," finding people "everywhere...doing penance in a thousand remarkable ways."

Walden is thus a kind of letter "to his kindred" at home ("poor students" perhaps), from a voyager who has been in strange and distant lands. The letter will be full of strange yet significant things about the Concord natives. Thoreau paradoxically identifies certain local areas in his distant lands as the shops, offices, and fields of Concord, but all contained in the idea of a long Pacific trading voyage from Salem or Boston to a land as far away as the Sandwich Islands and China, which is to say, into the mind and spirit of man and the quality of human life.

That the traveler who sends his *Walden* account home is a New England trader engaged in a trading voyage, is confirmed by the long maritime passage a third of the way along in the same ("Economy") section. Here he specifically associates himself with the long-flourishing, though already declining, China trade. This passage with its delicious and always noted irony, was composed for the first version of *Walden* and never altered therafter, and threfore seems to have attracted the later insertions of the beginning paragraphs already mentioned.

> I have always endeavored to acquire strict business habits. . . If your trade is with the Celestial Empire, then some small counting house on the coast, some Salem harbor, will be fixture enough. You will export such articles as the country affords. . . . These will be good ventures. To oversee all the details yourself in person; to be at once pilot and captain, and owner and underwriter. . . to be on all parts of the coast almost at the same time. . . to be your own telegraph, unweariedly sweeping the horizon, speaking all passing vessels bound coastwise. . . taking advantage of the results of all exploring expeditions, using new passages and all improvements in navigation;—Charts to be studied, the position of reefs and new lights and buoys to be ascertained, and ever and ever, the logarithmic tables to be corrected, for by the error of some calculator the vessel splits upon a rock that should have reached a friendly pier. . . studying the lives of the great discoverers and navigators, great adventurers and merchants, from Hanno and the Phoenicians down to our day. . . .
>
> I have thought that Walden Pond would be a good place for business. . . it is a good port and a good foundation. No Neva marshes to be filled; though you must everywhere build on piles of your own driving.

Thus he followed the trade routes of his mind and drove his mental pilings at the "Salem harbor" called Walden. It is the very trader-explorer additions, thus, that create a deliberate tone and shaping figure for the book. And as *Walden* opens, so it ends. In the great coda, Thoreau the explorer-trader has become a ruminating coastal sailor, and the voyaging into self, which has been reported throughout the book, is given its final turn, is underscored and driven home. In "Economy" he moves physically from Concord Village to Walden Pond in order to report on his discoveries among the "islands" of New England. In "Conclusion" he moves back (with appropriate and pungent recommendations) in quiet confidence and enjoyment toward a continuingly significant life. At Walden he went "before the mast and on the deck of the world" and prepared his long account to send back, admitting that sometimes he had been but a common sailor merely picking oakum. In the summing up, he is a curious sailor, a philosopher-explorer, who sometimes passenger-*like* gazes over the taffrail, but who rejects the privilege and ease of passengers. "I did not wish to take a cabin passage [the luxury of 'tradition and conformity' enjoyed by passengers], but rather to go before the mast and on the deck of the world, for there I could best see the moonlight on the mountains. I do not wish to go below now." He still chooses to be a participant in the work of navigation, an expert active *forecastle* man.[9] He is the complete voyager outwardly moving through space but inwardly traveling "farther than all travelers." It is at this point that he reminds us that the universe is wider than our views of it. We normally indulge only in "great-circle sailing," going the shortest distance between two distant ports. Travel instead, he says, the "thousand regions in your mind yet undiscovered" and "direct your eye right inward...be expert in home-cosmography." Be a Columbus or a Cook to whole new inner worlds and continents. Sail over the horizon into the unknown. Be now not a trader but an explorer. He noted in his *Journal* (IV, 289) that men have circumnavigated the globe, "but how few have sailed out of sight of common sense." In *Walden* the idea is elaborated startlingly, until the navigator takes off from the shores of the Pacific and sails into the infinite void of space.

> Is not our own interior white on the chart?...explore your own higher latitudes...it is easier to sail many thousand miles through cold and storm and cannibals, in a government ship, with five hundred men and boys to assist one, than it is to explore the private sea, the Atlantic and Pacific Ocean of one's being alone....England and France, Spain and Portugal, Gold Coast and Slave Coast, all front on this private sea; but no bark from them has ventured out of sight on land....Explore thyself....Start now on that farthest western way, which does not pause at the Mississippi, or the Pacific...but leads on direct, a tangent to this sphere, summer and winter, day and night, sun down, moon down, and at last earth down.

At many other points along the way in *Walden,* we are reminded that he is on a long voyage. In "Where I Lived and What I Lived For" the merchant ship shares with the ant and the railroad the task of illuminating the great "simplify, simplify" passage, his ringing challenge to a life of frittering. But it is the voyage image that stands emphatically framed by the words "simplicity, simplicity, simplicity" immediately before it and "simplify, simplify" immediately after it: "In the midst of this chopping sea of civilized life, such are the clouds and storms and quicksands and thousand-and-one items to be allowed for, that man has to live, if he would not founder and go to the bottom and not make his port at all, by dead reckoning, and he must be a great calculator indeed who succeeds."[10]

Also, the very cabin itself at Walden was a merchant ship bearing intellectual freight; and sometimes Thoreau felt cramped in it. It was difficult to get a sufficient distance from his guests when they began to utter big thoughts in big words. "You want room for thoughts to get into sailing trim and run a course or two before they make their port." Again,

"Ah! such discourse we had, hermit and philosopher, and the old settler... we three,—it expanded and racked my little house... it opened its seams so that they had to be caulked with much dullness there-after to stop the consequent leak, but I had enough of that kind of oakum already picked." And yet he felt satisfied on the whole. He could do what he came to do: actively explore his mind. He "had withdrawn so far within the great ocean of solitude, into which all the rivers of society empty, that for the most part, so far as my needs were concerned, only the finest sediment was deposited around me. Besides, there were wafted to me evidence of unexplored and uncultivated continents on the other side."[11]

In a longish passage from "The Pond in Winter," thoughts themselves become ships or navigators; and the inner sea becomes a cove or bay, sometimes landlocked. In this passage Thoreau first discusses how real sandbars are built up and what their relations are to adjacent shores and depth of water. Then he proceeds to apply this to the building up of a figurative sandbar from the swirls of spiritual seas, until the individual mind, or even a single thought, is isolated and "cut off from the ocean, wherein the thought secures its own conditions,—changes, perhaps, from salt to fresh, becomes a sweet sea, dead sea, or marsh."[12] This seems to invert the usual metaphor and make freshwater anchorage or stagnation (not salt-sea voyaging) of supreme value. But as though loath to relinquish the active sea figure, Thoreau closes the long discussion with two sentences that draw the figure back toward the ocean navigator seeking such a harbor.

> At the advent of each individual into this life, may we not suppose that such a bar has risen to the surface somewhere? It is true, we are such poor navigators that our thoughts, for the most part, stand off and on upon a harborless coast, are conversant only with the bights of the bays of poesy, or steer for the public ports of entry, and go into the dry docks of science, where they merely refit for this world, and no natural currents concur to individualize them.

The figure of the long sea voyage, which is structurally and poetically so important in the *Week* and *Walden,* functions in an interesting passage on winter in the *Journal,* written a little over a month before he was to be reading the first page-proofs for *Walden.* For a modern reader it lies beneath the surface and appears more subtle than it would to mid nineteenth-century readers. It is suggested at the beginning and the end of the passage, enclosing a bristling array of other metaphors and tending to unify them. The passage is worth looking at, furthermore, because it has been misread and consequently misapplied on a subject of great importance to Thoreau: winter and thinking. As thinking was for him the most important function of man ("There is no more Herculean task than to think a thought about this life and then get it well expressed"), and as the long hearth-hugging winter seemed divinely appointed for it. Thoreau's many remarks on winter warrant attention.

It is misleading to assume, as some have, that he merely suffered winter Spartan-like because he complained that November 13, 1851, a cold, dark, and depressing day, was "such a day as will almost oblige a man to eat his own heart," or because three years later he confided that January was "the hardest month to get through," adding (imagining himself to be a mariner), "When you have weathered that, you get into the gulf-stream of winter, nearer the shores of spring." The fact is that for twenty years Thoreau treasured winter as the season for intellectual work. In winter, he wrote in October of 1851, "man migrates into his mind," a more intense intellectual activity (reading, remembering, and thinking "high in [his] chamber") being afforded by the season of lessened physical activity and the long evenings indoors. "The alert and energetic man leads a more intellectual life in winter than in summer. In summer the animal and vegetable in him are perfected as in a torrid zone; he lives in his senses mainly. In winter cold reason and not warm passion has her sway; he lives in thought and reflection. . . ." Man fails if he curls up like the marmot or the chipmunk. The migration into mind is "to perpetual summer. And to a healthy man the winter of his discontent never comes."[13] Two weeks later, depressed by a feeling that the strings of his being were not vibrating satisfactorily to divine winds, he repeats the sanative thought: "Winter, with its *inwardness* is upon us. A man is constrained to sit down, and to think."[14] Apparently he did so, and worked especially hard at his *Journal,* reminding himself that when "the thermometer is down to 20°, the streams of thought tinkle underneath" impelling him to "let all things give way to the impulse of expression."[15] Then he draws a strict analogy between farmer and scholar. In summer each digs peat and muck and gets them up. In winter each carts off "virgin loads of fertilizing soils" and brings them into the barnyard. "My barnyard is my journal."[16] The "virgin loads" are the material by means of which in winter "we will think brave and hardy and most native thoughts."[17] Winter and intense intellectual work with both vegetable muck and oily yield were associations of long standing.

With winter occupying thus a well-defined place in the calendar of Thoreau's intellectual life, his emerging nautical metaphor for it is of great interest. Continuing in a major *Journal* entry (January 30, 1854) we find a significant elaboration of the theme (emphases are mine):

> Winter, cold and *bound out* as it is, is thrown to us like a bone to a famishing dog, and we are expected to get the marrow out of it. . .the winter was not given to us for no purpose. We must thaw its

> cold with our genialness. We are tasked to find out all the nutriment it yields. If it is a cold and hard season, its fruit, no doubt, is the more concentrated and nutty. It took the cold and bleakness of November to ripen the walnut, but the human brain is the kernel which the winter itself matures. . . . Then is the great harvest of the year, the *harvest of thought.* All previous harvests are stubble to this, mere fodder and green crop. Now we burn with purer flame like the stars; *our oil is winter-strained.* We are islanded in Atlantic and Pacific and Indian *Oceans of thought,* Bermudas, or Friendly or Spice Islands.[18]

This energetic statement reminds us that for whalers, South Sea traders, and philosopher-artists winter is the great working season. A bone to a famishing dog is a *good* thing. Winter promises the possibility of oily yield from bone marrow, ripened nuts, whale oil, and the human mind. The South Sea voyage metaphor, stressing the bound out-ness of both Thoreau and the whalers, frames and unifies the paragraph.

The next day was unexpectedly warm in Concord, but Thoreau was still on his voyage. The snow melted in the sun, and the people in the Thoreau household, warming to it, commented on signs of spring. But Thoreau wrote, "But I do not melt;. . . I am bound out still."[19] He had some winter thinking yet to do. The following spring (1855) a similar sudden warm day at the end of March affected him similarly, and he underscored "*bound out,*" revealing his adoption of the phrase by then as his personal and habitual expression for winter's "inwardness."

Conversely "getting in" symbolized spring, the return from winter voyages, sailing deep with cargo and returning to home, friends, and the luxury of stimulating sense experience ashore. In the spring of 1859 while Thoreau was still revising and reworking "Autumnal Tints," he wrote, "This first sight of the bare tawny russet earth. . . affects me as the first glimpse of land, his native land, does the voyager who has not seen it in a long time."[20] And again, "The air is more genial, laden with the fragrance of spring flowers. I, sailing in the spring ocean, getting in from my winter voyage, begin to smell the land. . . . I draw near the land; I begin to lie down and stretch myself. After my winter voyage I begin to smell the land."[21] The metaphor, therefore, that he clings to for winter and the Herculean task of thinking a thought about life and expressing it is that of a Salem or Boston or New Bedford sea captain's voyage, *out* in the winter, *in* in the spring. We shall see how this nautical cycle is again remarkably effectively in the central figure in "Autumnal Tints."

From the February day in 1838 when Thoreau identified himself with the trader-philosopher Zeno, who "stood in precisely the same relationship to the world as I do now," to the day in February of 1859 when he sat in the stillness of winter and heard "only the sound of the surf on our internal seas," he felt poetic kinship with ocean navigators; and like the practical philosopher Zeno, he sailed on. The record of Thoreau's intellectual growth and lifelong quest can be read in his voyage figures alone. During his Harvard days he saw himself as a solitary voyager searching for he knew not what. "I may be away to Singapoor by the next tide," he wrote to a classmate. In 1839 he was beginning to understand that "There is a *terra firma* in society as well as in geography, some [of] whose ports you may make by dead reckoning in all weather."[22] Near the end of his life he rebuffed fools and made his eloquent plea for living in the present. "You must live in the present, launch yourself on every wave, find your eternity in each moment. Fools stand on their island opportunities and look toward another land. There is no other land; there is no other life but this...Let us see vessels sailing prosperously before the wind, and not simply stranded barks."[23]

In other words, the significant life is a life of steady onward motion. Though a man may at times yearn to reach some desired shore or quiet port, he knows that the cape or headland may never be rounded nor the distant shore ever be reached. Infinity cannot be de-fined. The seeker always seeks, and instead of scaling Alps on Alps of knowledge as with Alexander Pope, he sails past ever new landmarks. This is why the ending of *Walden* is so important. So long as he stays on the deck of the world and sails, he can continue the mental life in a series of lives, or "one world at a time" in a universe of worlds. The one exception is the inevitable final voyage home, laden deep with products of his thinking—the controlling figure, as we shall see, in "Autumnal Tints."

Sometimes he had great difficulty in navigating the winter days, as in January, "the hardest month to get through." In February he felt he had "more sea-room in the day" without so much danger of running aground on the two promontories of morning and evening. "It is a narrow pass, and you must go through with the tide." In such conceits the narrow passage is commonly between mountains or icebergs or masses of floe ice. He could not actually go on a northwest passage, he once said, so he "would find a passage round the actual world where I am." He would "connect the Behring Straits and Lancaster Sounds of thought; winter on Melville Island, and make a chart of Banks Land; explore the northward trending Wellington Inlet, where there is said to be a perpetual open sea, cutting my way through floes of ice."[24]

Navigation of the inner inner sea haunted his dreams. One evening in October of 1851 Thoreau was reading an account of the voyages of the Norsemen. That night he had a remarkable dream. On the level of personal meaning related to immediate life, it shows as vividly as anything he wrote his awareness of the influence of profound psychic forces upon him—of sailing the ocean of his being, and of divine influences playing upon him. It is Coleridgean both in an expression of keen regret and in the concept of the body as a musical instrument, the familiar Romantic Aeolian harp. It is Wordsworthian in its recognition of the mystical identity of the ocean with the true spiritual nature of man. It is a dream sequence of raw materials for conscious poetic rendering.

> I awoke this morning to infinite regret. In my dream I had been riding, but the horses bit each other...and it was my employment to hold their heads apart. Next I sailed over the sea in a small vessel such as the Northmen used, as it were to the Bay of Fundy, and thence overland I sailed, still over the shallows about the sources of rivers toward the deeper *channel* of a stream which emptied into the Gulf beyond,—the Miramichi was it? Again I was in my own small pleasure-boat, learning to sail on the sea, and I raised my sail before my anchor, which I dragged far into the sea. I saw the buttons which had come off the coats of drowned men, and suddenly I saw my dog—when I knew not that I had one—standing in the sea up to his chin, to warm his legs, which had been wet, which the cool wind numbed.[25]

This dream continues with a scene in the Concord meadows where Thoreau and Alcott quote "grand and pleasing" couplets to one another. It ends with a vivid impression as he wakens that he had just been functioning as a divinely-playing musical instrument.

> I heard a strain die out,—a bugle, or a clarionet, or a flute. My body was the organ and channel of melody....I awoke, therefore, to an infinite regret...to find myself not the thoroughfare of glorious and world-stirring inspirations, but a scuttle full of dirt....I heard the last strain or flourish...played on my body as the instrument. Such I knew I had been and might be again, and my regret arose from the consciousness how little like a musical instrument my body was now.

Nowhere else does Thoreau reveal such interesting complexities in the inner sea figure. Its shifting scenes tell us how deeply he felt about the psychic realities he more optimistically presents to the reader in the spirit of ongoingness in the Conclusion to *Walden.* Fragilely held together by the device of the voyage, they lead from the uncontrolled energies of the biting horses to the pleasing couplets of poets in a sweet meadow, from the sturdy and divinely responsive sailor to the discouraged though not despairing poet. As a statement of pathetic loss, it is companion to Thoreau's better known symbols: the hound, the bay horse, and the turtle dove.

The general impression created by the account of this dream, is a feeling first of extent and scope, as Thoreau, imagining himself a Norseman, sails over both sea and land. That is, everywhere. Over land or in the shallows he is nevertheless seeking the deepest parts, the "*channel,*" the importance of which is stressed by Thoreau's own italics. Next he is in his own boat far out to sea, learning deepwater navigation though continuing to drag his anchor in spiritual shallows. The verse recitations with Alcott return him to shallow places over which he had often sailed—the Concord meadows. Though the couplets of other poets which the men are reciting please them, they are poor things, as suggested by the dryness all around them. There is *no* depth of water here, in contrast to those flood stages when Thoreau sailed over them on innumerable voyages. From the image of himself as Norse explorer, then, to that of the played-upon musical instrument, the progression is more and more toward the intensely personal, until it ends in the ecstasy of remembered musical response to the winds of the infinite, and finally the infinite regret at the loss of that divine music as he wakens. Here in the last part of the dream the return to the word "channel" and the repetition of "thorough-fare," both used as equivalents for both seaways and the hollow parts of a wind instrument, help to contain all the events within the voyage framework.[26]

The significant word "channel" has had a long history in Thoreau's thinking and had become metaphorically fixed. Expanding a line from Ben Jonson about the evil man who "makes himself a thorough-fare of vice," he had in March of 1841 played with the idea of channels and thoroughfares as applied to moral and creative aspects of man's life. The next month and on into May of that crucial year of self-examination, five entries in his *Journal* repeat the channel image. In April he was sure a man's life "will cut its own channel." In May, "though a ridge intervene, I have but to see, or make, a gap to the sea." He was lengthening the time he had expressed earlier which called for all men to "be at the helm at least once a day" to the equivalent of being there all the time. In November of 1850 he recorded his desire to make himself "the thoroughfare of thrilling thoughts, live all that can be lived." Some months later he had the Norseman dream. It is apparent that Thoreau was consciously moving from a position of relative stasis (quiet floating and musing, vague awareness of "sphere music" from some not fully comprehended Aeolian harp outside him) to a position of stressing intellectual and creative effort here and now, of choosing a vocation, and of realizing that man can cut his *own* channel and *be* that Aeolian harp.

By the early 1850's he has settled on his vocation—a life of thought and literary expression. He ruefully recognizes that he is only a few steps away from his youthful mystical intensity. He is reading Coleridge and Wordsworth, pondering Wordsworth's theme in the ode of immortality" of the price one pays for maturing. He is facing up at some cost to the fact, or as Sherman Paul puts it in "The Wise Silence," "He had discovered...that the quality of insight depends on the quality of mind." His quest has turned more emphatically earthward, to the place where he could "dwell as near as possible to the channel in which my life flows."[27] He demands that the whole man be involved. "It is essential," he wrote in March of 1853, "that a man confine himself to pursuits—a scholar, for instance, to studies—which lie next to and conduce to his life...to the experience or life of the senses." By this time Thoreau is composing *Walden* and is putting well seasoned images together in his concluding appeal to all men to search for new continents and worlds within, "opening new channels, not of trade, but of thought."

Seeming to lie always at hand, the metaphor of the strong navigator was easily suited to strong men among Thoreau's contemporaries. Though he felt that the works of Thomas Carlyle "indicated a depth...which he neglects to fathom," and that Carlyle was more an actor than a thinker, Thoreau felt his works were the richest cargo "the packets have brought over to us...the best apology for all the bustle and sin of commerce," each idea and mannerism stamped with Carlyle's own stamp. And although he objects also that Carlyle merely "indicated a depth...which he neglects to fathom," and does not quite do what "the universe expects every man to do...in his parallel of latitude," he obviously relished him as a courageous mental navigator like himself, not bounded by ordinary courses and limits. In so doing he enlarged a metaphor of Carlyle as an exporter-importer of ideas across the English Channel, into a bold transatlantic voyager pushing westward to new lands, the metaphor he re-employed in *Cape Cod.*

What in a writer of less breadth would have been the proposition which would have bounded his discourse, his column of victory, his Pillar of Hercules, and *ne plus ultra,* is in Carlyle frequently the same thought unfolded, no Pillar of Hercules, but a considerable prospect, north and south, along the Atlantic coast. There are other pillars of Hercules, like beacons and lighthouses, still further in the horizon, toward Atlantis, set up by a few ancient and modern travelers; but so far as this traveler goes, he clears and colonizes, and all the surplus population of London is bound hither at once.[28]

It might have been predicted that Thoreau would see the vigorous New Hampshire abolitionist editor, Nathaniel P. Rogers, whom he likened to Carlyle, as an adventurous navigator also. Thoreau had never met the man, but it was enough for him to admire Rogers from a distance because of his courageous stand against the abolitionists' societies, which action drew upon him calumny and persecution. So Thoreau wrote in the *Dial* for April, 1844: At his desk at the *Herald of Freedom* he is "no civil pilot sitting aft" waiting for news. This editor is "wide awake, and standing on the beak of his ship...a Yankee sealer, who makes those unexplored continents his harbors in which to refit for more adventurous cruises."[29]

And finally, images of ocean navigator are favorites in Thoreau's poems.[30] Sometimes, as in "With Frontier Strength..." and "To the Comet," his eye is on ordinary physical objects. In the former poem one third of the hundred lines celebrate the strength and deep-carrying holds of a fleet of ships of the line convoying clouds westward, referring to the Peterborough Hills. This picture of mountains as ships, Henry W. Wells has already observed, "possesses a poetic scope and richness of imagination of which Emerson proved incapable."[31] The comet is neatly imaged as a "celestial privateer" sculling without a sail. Of far greater interest, however, are the poems of poignant personal feeling, in which—as in *Walden*—the navigator is Thoreau. He has reminded us that his poems are exterior manifestations of the poet's "very private history," his biography in fact. They are not to be taken lightly, therefore.

The fascinating poem "The Departure" is a good instance. In it he plaintively commemorates his departure from the Emerson household (probably in 1843). He has "ridden" in the Emerson roadstead, been a "stranger moored" to the Emerson pier, enjoyed the olive and the vine and all that the land afforded; yet he has freighted no "argosy." But more and more the sullen waves had come rolling to the shore, and in his discontent he

...unfurled his mast
To receive the fragrant blast,
And that same freshening gale
Which woo'd him to remain
Again and again—
It was that filled his sail
And drove him to the main.

All day long the low hung clouds
Dropt tears into the sea
And the wind amid the shrouds
Sighed plaintively.[32]

Embedded in the ninth or tenth paragraph of the late (1863) lecture-essay *Life Without Principle* lies the striking and now familiar figure which he presses upon us as an image of his whole life as a sentient being. He is here a New England sea captain rather than a questing Ulysses, achieving thereby the special homespun effectiveness that has made it memorable. Perhaps it may be quoted here with somewhat more than its normal effect.

> I have been surprised when one has with confidence proposed to me, a grown man, to embark in some enterprise of his, as if I had absolutely nothing to do, my life having been a complete failure hitherto. What a doubtful compliment this, to pay me! As if he had met me half way across the ocean beating up against the wind, but bound nowhere and proposed to me to go along with him! If I did, what do you think the underwriters would say? No, no! I am not without employment at this stage of the voyage. To tell the truth I saw an advertisement for able-bodied seamen, when I was a boy, sauntering in my native port, and as soon as I came of age I embarked.

Homeric Indiaman

Flaunt out, O sea, your separate flags of nations!
...and for the soul of man one flag above all the rest
A spiritual woven signal for all nations, emblem of man elate above death,

Token of all brave captains and all intrepid sailors and mates.

Whitman, *Song for All Seas, All Ships*

Perhaps the time will come when we shall not be content to go back and forth upon a raft to some Homeric or Shakespearean Indiaman that lies upon a reef.

Walden

VII

Homeric Indiaman

THE GREAT WESTWARD-SAILING NAVIGATORS stirred the imagination of Thoreau not only for their qualities of strength, endurance, courage, and the like, but for the simple reason as well that they sailed west to a new world. Unlike the painter Thomas Cole in his five panels called "The Progress of Empire" (1836), or James Fenimore Cooper in his Robinson-Crusoe-Utopian novel *The Crater* (1822), Thoreau emphasized the positive aspects of the Westward Movement of European man. Like Whitman he entertained that highest, best aspect of the American dream having little to do with riches but much to do with a greater, healthier, newer society, the hope and possibility of a race of freer and nobler men who were, as Thoreau said, "not content to go back and forth on a raft" salvaging goods from their cultural past. Whitman viewed the movement as a great surging tide, irresistible, destined, exalting. Thoreau presented it as a stirring possibility and an invitation to individual men who through struggle, self-examination, and sometimes chance, found themselves on new ground, not as flotsam nor yet as empire builders, but as creative beings, as mariners-terreners whose inner voyages could be as significant as their outward journeys across the vastness of America.

Among the European navigators whom Thoreau admired (Columbus, Raleigh, and others) was strangely enough Robinson Crusoe. His veneration of the historical figures was explicit and recurring, and has often been noted. The full extent of his regard for the world's most famous fictional castaway has not. To be sure, Defoe's novel has been readily bracketed with *Gulliver's Travels* and *Pilgrim's Progress* as one of three literary prototypes of *Walden.*[1] Crusoe was alone on his island; Thoreau was alone at Walden. And for fifty years a standard *History of American Literature* has carried the astonishing remark that "it is the adventurous Robinson Crusoe part of *Walden* that is imperishable." The implication is that economic self-sufficiency is what *Walden* is all about. Although we do not read *Walden* with such an emphasis now, and although Thoreau certainly had Crusoe in mind at Walden Pond, he saw him as far more than an ingenious and resourceful fictional castaway and rough prototype of himself at one moment in his life.

Crusoe represented that antique or "Homeric" quality in men of the New World of which F. O. Matthiessen speaks, a quality that linked their genius for work with the perennial basic experience of the race. He represented man forever coping and forever groping. He furthermore symbolized fresh beginnings, standing for Man, infinite in faculty, shedding false sophistication and acquiring "wildness," man refreshed from having been stripped, facing even as we today finally and desperately face the challenge of putting man in such a relation to the universe that the survival and regeneration of a gifted terrestrial race may be possible. With us it is a grim necessity; with Thoreau it was a thrilling and perennial possibility. An expanded and fairly complicated metaphor of shipwreck has much to do with it.

Most readers of the first sections of *Walden* are of course easily reminded of Robinson Crusoe.[2] The enormous and exaggerated stress on solitary life and on the problems of mere subsistence are only too apparent. Even though the thoughtful reader may wonder about any thoroughgoing sympathetic kinship between Thoreau and Crusoe because of Crusoe's bland acceptance of money values, of British colonial expansion, and of unquestioned supremacy of Puritan-Christian religious faith (all antipathetic to Thoreau),[3] yet the reader is led by Thoreau in *Walden* and elsewhere to look at the famous castaway positvely. Thoreau ultimately fastens on him as symbolic of a universal quest, the quest for a hard won, worthy life. In the Sunday section of the *Week,* he asserts that Crusoe is mythic.

"All men are children, and of one family," he writes. "The same tale sends them all to bed, and wakes them in the morning." When the Arabians had read a translation of *Robinson Crusoe* furnished them by Joseph Wolff, a missionary, they exclaimed, "'Oh, that Robinson Crusoe must have been a great prophet!'" His adventures and wisdom were believed, he repeats from Wolff.[4] This is Thoreau's illustration of a fable in the process of becoming myth. The passage goes on to say that tales "migrate from east to west, and again from west to east." Having become myths, they contain only "enduring and essential truth," the "thoughts and dreams of men" addressing men as yet unborn. "Who knows what shape the fable of Columbus will at length assume," or even, he says, that of Benjamin Franklin, of whom later generations may declare, he "aided the Americans to gain their independence, instructed mankind in economy, and drew down lightning from the clouds." Penetrating the humor of this remark, F.O. Matthiessen recognized that "Thoreau's ability to create myth ran on a deeper level than his amused fancies about Franklin."[5] At Walden, for example, he explains Thoreau was actually concerned in re-creating a basic myth—the union of work and culture. Columbus and Crusoe ran on this deeper level.

When Thoreau came to write the late essay, "Walking," his brief excursion into speculation had deepened into conviction regarding the significance of the whole American hemisphere. The West was "wild and free," product of the pristine vigors still to be found in the rich valleys of the great rivers of both the Americas, from the Plate, the Amazon, and the Orinoco in the South to the Mississippi and the St. Lawrence in the North. The West was "preparing to add its fables to those of the East."

It is not surprising, therefore, to find that Defoe's famous mariner lurked in Thoreau's mind at odd and interesting moments, as when he spent many leisurely days searching for the appropriate site for his famous experiment in living. The site could have been half a dozen places other than Walden Pond. It had to be some spot close to "the perennial source of our life" where he could dig his cellar and have some horizon to his life. He considered isolated farms and islands and ramshackle huts. Before he decided on Walden, he had cast his eye on the old Hollowell Farm, so amusingly "owned" then returned to the owner, and described in "Where I Lived and What I Lived For" in *Walden*. "The present [Walden] was my next experiment in this kind." As he gave back the farm, he kept the landscape for himself and punningly appropriated the first two lines of William Cowper's poem on Alexander Selkirk, whose claim to fame rests on the fact that he was the prototype of the fictional Crusoe.

I am monarch of all I *survey*.
My right there is none to dispute.

Thoreau has Crusoe in mind here, not Selkirk. With no hesitation he accepts the confusion of Crusoe with Selkirk that the world has accepted ever since Cowper himself merged the language of Defoe's novel with the figure of an actually marooned man.[6] Indeed the point of view in the whole poem is that of Crusoe.[7]

Before the Hollowell Farm Thoreau had looked at the Baker Farm and others. He also glanced longingly at uninhabited islands. Though he boasted, "Wherever I sat, there I might live," yet we know "every spot" was not possible for the kind of residence he wanted. Such a place must have "complete retirement" where he might live "free and uncommitted." Six years before he went to Walden he had been high up on the Merrimac River with his brother, where in the neighborhood of the Souhegan River and Amoskeag he had canvassed the river islands, which the boys always preferred over the river bank for camping spots. "An island always pleases my imagination, even the smallest, as a small continent and integral part of the globe. I have a fancy for building my hut on one."[8] Islands symbolized for him thought, thoughts continents, or even "some continent man" who was far off and difficult to reach but, like the perfect friend, worth navigating toward. Unlike John Donne, Thoreau thought every man *was* an island, and every island held enormous potential for man, a more interesting place than a farm. But he finally went to Walden Pond, and the book he wrote came to be called "Walden" instead of "Amoskeag," "Hollowell," or "Fairhaven."

Among the many roles he imagined for himself on the Merrimac (explorer, deep-water sailor, *voyageur*, and so on) was also that of Robinson Crusoe. At the precise place where he gazed at and commented on islands, he and his brother encountered a few miles above Amoskeag young Nathan, a New England farm boy who in turn gazed longingly at them. A "little flaxen-haired boy, with some tradition, or small edition, of Robinson Crusoe in his head, who had been charmed by the account of our adventures, and asked his father's permission to join us.... He was a lively and interesting boy." And the two Crusoes "would have been glad to ship him," responding with warmth to his fancies.

It is in keeping with such a state of mind that Robinson Crusoe came to Thoreau's mind when the waters of the Concord River on a warm Sunday morning in May of 1857 seemed transformed into South Sea shores, islands, and bays; he was impelled to cruise off three shores at once: those of Concord, South America, and himself. "What fair isles, what remote coast shall we explore? What San Salvador or Bay of All Saints arrive at? All isles seem fortunate and blessed." The men and boys he saw going forth in boats were "voyagers;" but men and boys who stayed ashore and in their new clothes sat in straight-backed church pews in subjection. Worshipping neither Thor nor Christ, Thoreau sympathized "rather with the boy who has none to look after him.... I met such a boy...with bare feet and pants rolled up.... Better for him to read 'Robinson Crusoe' than Baxter's 'Saints' Rest'."[9]

Knowing his frame of mind, therefore, in his preliminary searches, we accept parallels between activities of Thoreau at Walden Pond and Crusoe on his Island of Despair. They seem at first perhaps more fortuitous and more immediately diverting than significant. Indeed, Thoreau's meticulous itemizing of details of house-building and domestic economy in *Walden must* be taken lightly, as no one today doubts that Thoreau himself was amused. They constitute another example of his "extra-vagance." It is even tempting to think he might be mimicking Defoe. He overloads his account. Starting with only a few tools, he pares life down to the essentials that Robinson Crusoe was forced to begin with: the clearing of the land; the cultivation of a garden, including the various kinds of seeds he uses, which crops succeed, which fail; the construction of a house; the exact amount of such things as boards, nails, hinges, screws, and one thousand old bricks. The early chapters overwhelm us with details. This is precisely Defoe's trick. Other parallels are: the cutting of timber, the salvage of iron, wood, and brick from other, disused structures; careful selection of the homesite; the difficulties of making pots, baking bread, etc. Piece by piece their houses are displayed as they go up.

Both men compile journals. Crusoe's "Journal" was a solemn detailing of fact and event, for the most part a retrospective record, a mariner's log. Thoreau's own monumental work of art was a repository of his finest thinking and acutest observation. They are vastly different, but in describing all the business of building and settling in at Walden, Thoreau often comes close to the matter-of-fact style of Crusoe. "December 11," Crusoe set down, "This day I went to work with it accordingly, and got two shores or posts pitched upright to the top with two pieces of boards across over each post. This I finished the next day; and setting more posts up with boards, in about a week more I had the roof secured; and the posts standing in rows, served for partitions to part of my house." Thoreau writes in *Walden*, "I began to occupy my house on the 4th of July, as soon as it was boarded and roofed, for the boards were carefully featheredged and lapped, so that it was perfectly impervious to rain, but before boarding I laid the foundation of a chimney at one end, bringing two cartloads of stones up the hill from the pond in my arms." Like Crusoe, Thoreau built his house on the side of a hill which sloped toward and gave a view of the water. They both dug a cave-like cellar out of the hillside. All in all they created their establishments "out of the necessities and character of the indweller, who is the only builder."[10]

Inevitable parallels in thought and action also appear. Thoreau went to the woods, as every one knows, "to front only the essential facts of life, and see if I could not learn what it had to teach...to drive life into a corner, and reduce it to its lowest terms, and, if it proved to be mean, why then to get the whole and genuine meanness of it...or if it were sublime, to know it by experience." Robinson Crusoe not only labored at the practical essentials, but meditated the whole meaning of life, especially as he lay sick. "What is this earth and sea.... And what am I, and all other creatures, wild and tame, human and brutal, whence are we?" Crusoe's meditations led him to Divine Providence; Thoreau's to God-like man. Crusoe was driven to religious essentials; Thoreau to essentials of the human spirit. Such thoughts brought them both to a similar plane with regard to the luxuries of civilization: "All the good things of this world are no farther good to us than they are for our use," as Crusoe put it.[11]

Both men thought long on the subject of solitude, and devoted large sections of their respective books to the subject, though Crusoe's come principally in Defoe's second and third volumes, after the island episode.[12] Thus is appears that Crusoe, like Thoreau, faced far more than the struggle for survival and subsistence. They both faced themselves and struggled with the meaning of life. Each has much to say about exploring the inner sea. Furthermore, it should not be forgotten that Crusoe, too, passed through a rebirth or re-intensification of spirit on the island at the time of his grievous sickness—for him a deeply religious, if only momentary, experience and a direct result of his solitary life.

Both *Robinson Crusoe* and *Walden* generate excitement in us because in them we get to the root of things. Crusoe and Thoreau recognize the connection between the life they are leading and the idea of getting back to the primitive source of things. Crusoe says, "I fancied myself now like one of the ancient giants which were said to live in caves and holes in rocks where none could come at them. . . ."[13] Thoreau links his own life with that of primitive man, with the Golden Age of Greece, Adam and Eve, the fall of Troy, with Ulysses and by extension with the earlier history of his own town. At Walden both time and place were changed, and he "dwelt nearer to those parts of the universe which most attracted" him. Both Crusoe and Thoreau in some sense, as Sherman Paul remarks in connection with Thoreau,[14] retrace the history of civilization and look at its accomplishments with innocent eyes. In Crusoe Thoreau saw a man who *heroically* began from scratch.

There are thus numerous parallels and teasingly suggestive philosophical points of overlap. That Thoreau at Walden is thinking specifically of himself as Crusoe is seen when we meet the mention of the notched stick. "In any weather, and at any hour of the day or night I have been anxious to improve the nick of time and notch it on my stick, too," he wrote, modifying only slightly his *Journal* entry of February 22, 1841, which had ended, "as Robinson Crusoe on his stick." A few paragraphs later, on the subject of changing taste in man's clothing, Crusoe's famous goatskin hat lurks behind Thoreau's ilustration of headpieces, combining primitive hats of tropical and temperate climes in the single picture of change: "gradually leaving off the palm-leaf hat or cap of woodchuck skin."[15]

At Walden or anywhere else when he felt alone, Thoreau recalled Robinson Crusoe. "There goes a rumor," he wrote in the *Week* on the impossibility of even finding a perfect friend, "that the earth is inhabited, but the ship-wrecked mariner has not seen a footprint in the sand." When a feeling of utter loneliness once overwhelmed him while he walked in the late November woods, a nuthatch called out, "Nay, nay!" and re-established contact with the world of living things. In his loneliness Thoreau had just complained, "Not even a man Friday remains." The nuthatch was his Friday, without benefit of footprint. And among those early speculations concerning places where he might live or roles he might play in life, one list ends, "or a Robinson Crusoe in the Pacific, or a silent navigator of any sea. So wide the choice of parts, what a pity if the part of

Hamlet be left out!"[16] Five years after he wrote this, he combined Hamlet and Crusoe at Walden Pond.

The world remembers certain vivid scenes and episodes from Robinson Crusoe's famous island adventure: the shipwreck, the raft, the stockade, the clothing made of skins, the parrot, the making of a small boat, the footprint in the sand, and Friday. These have all passed into the public domain and live a life of their own. Thoreau freely appropriated them. At Walden he was amused at the parallels between himself and Crusoe. At all times he responded with vigor to Crusoe's struggle for survival. But the most important meaning for Thoreau lay in that which was symbolized by the shipwreck, the salvage operation, and the building of a boat. For him these three belonged together, presenting his favorite figure of heroic man, naked, alone, and shorn of society's usual props, facing west, and overcoming in order to go on.

In his day Thoreau was close to a number of real shipwrecks, as we have seen, yet Robinson Crusoe's held a greater imaginative appeal than any other. The deaths of the Irish emigrants in the wreck of the *St. John* reported in *Cape Cod* elicited mainly a conventional analogy and a witty remark about funerals.[17] The finality of the event sealed it off from little more than a conventional death metaphor. The importance of the Crusoe shipwreck, however, is that the protagonist is a sole human being who stays alive, constructs a new life, and does indeed go on to new worlds, an experience of renewal. More importantly, Crusoe's shipwreck is distinguished by the great salvage operation, the rafting of goods ashore. This feature appealed strongly to Thoreau, judging from the number of times he mentions it. For example, he wrote to Harrison Blake in 1852 that as for passing through and rising above any great and glorious experience, "I cannot say I even sailed so creditably." As moral sailor, he had "fallen behind by whole continents of virtue.... But I trust...that, with a stiff wind, some Friday, when I have thrown some of my cargo overboard, I may make up for all that distance lost. Perhaps the time will come when we shall not be content to go back and forth to some Homeric or Shakespearean Indiaman that lies upon a reef, but build a bark out of that wreck and others that lie in the sands of this desolate island...in which to sail away to whole worlds of light and life...." Five years after he had written this (three years after Walden), he entered in his *Journal*, "My planks and timbers are scattered. At most I hope to make a sort of raft of Friendship, on which, with a few of our treasures, we may float to some firm land."[18]

It seems likely, therefore, that the wrecked Robinson Crusoe lay in the back of his mind also when he presented his retrospective account in the Tuesday section of the *Week* of an acute private adventure at the summit of Saddleback Mountain. It was early morning and the "terrestrial world" was blotted out by the "varied swell" of the mist clouds below, leaving the drifting solitary observer to muse upon the elavation of his mind and spirit that corresponded to a physical elevation intensified by the dropping out of the familiar earth. It was a cleansing, regenerating experience in which he was floating toward "some firm land."

> As the light increased, I discovered around me an ocean of mist, which by chance reached up exactly to the base of the tower, and shut out every vestige of the earth, while I was left floating on this fragment of the wreck of a world, on my carved plank, in cloudland; a situation which required no aid from the imagination to render it impressive. As the light in the east steadily increased, it revealed to me more clearly the new world into which I had risen in the night, the new *terra firma* perchance of my future life.

These bits of "exaggerated history" (his phrase in the *Journal* for poetry) were "truth referred to a new standard." Or, as elsewhere, calling history "facts," he stressed the use to which facts may be put—a mere frame for his picture, "material to the mythology." "I would so state the facts that they shall be significant, shall be mythic or mythologic."[19]

Responding poetically to the "fact" of the wrecked Crusoe, Thoreau saw an enlarged symbol of the best the New World had to offer. As castaway, Crusoe endured. As a solitary, he survived. But above all he held promise of becoming that new "Columbus to whole continents and worlds within." He comes near to being Thoreau's complete man, though the picture of hardy mariner is never allowed to fade. Crusoe was free from the past. He had "the callous palms of the laborer" which are "conversant with the finer tissues of self-respect and heroism, whose touch thrills the heart."[20] He was capable of the inner struggles of thought. He was furthermore a man in motion, traveling toward a potentially even more creative life, the kind of man who *could* put foundations under aircastles. In such a frame of reference he related Robinson Crusoe to his "new standard," the heroic.

In today's language used to describe the nineteenth century American dream, Crusoe was in Thoreau's eyes the old Adam thrown down on a new shore but endowed with powers enabling him to rise and create, not a new Eden, but a new greater Adam. Thus nothing casual or merely whimsical seems to have been responsible for associating the heroic qualities of Crusoe with those of Raleigh and Columbus. Unlike Clarel and his friends in Melville's *Clarel* who cried out,

> To Terminus build fanes!
> Columbus ended earth's romance:
> No New World to mankind remains!

Thoreau saw the westward migrants in quite opposite roles. He still had what Melville had lost, the vision of new beginnings. "We go westward as into the future, with a spirit of enterprise and adventure." The "Homeric" wreck, therefore, is symbolic of a single event in a vast and surging movement of society and in the mind of man, but operative through individual strong men, "This man who read his Homer in a hut by a woodland lake," as Odell Shephard wrote of Thoreau, "can show us better, perhaps, than any other teacher we have had yet how to coordinate whatever is peculiarly American with the tradition of the ages."[21]

Thoreau's Crusoe, symbolically conceived as relating to rebirth and renewal, takes his place with the crowing cockerel and the insect emerging from old apple wood. R.W.B. Lewis asserts in *The American Adam* that Thoreau was demanding "that individuals start life all over again, and that in the new world a fresh start was literally and immediately possible." Lewis notes further that though Thoreau sometimes began the process for himself by a return to childhood experience and scenes, he declared in maturity, "But now I made my home by the shore." Lewis implies that living by the shore is a step away from childhood, and because, in Thoreau's words, "every child begins the world again," it is desirable to go home again, back to the attitude of the child. "Renewal was a kind of homecoming. . . an impulse to return to the womb." Strictly with regard to re-*birth*, Lewis's figure holds. Thoreau, however, extended the idea of renewal in several directions. We have already seen how much he depended on the idea of the shore as the proper place for man's abode because man not only belongs on the land, but on the shore he is most favorably situated to achieve continuing and ever recurring spiritual reinvigoration. The moment presents more of a strong feeling of on-going than a returning.

Lewis encapsulates his remarks about Thoreau under the heading, "The Case Against the Past," which is to say the case is for the future. Thoreau's myth of Robinson Crusoe is indeed concerned with the pulsations of man's renewal. As an extraordinarily endowed creature existing in nature, man always has the power to stand on some new shore. "The morning hope is soon lost in what becomes the routine of the day, and we do not recover ourselves until we land on the pensive shores of the evening, shores which skirt the great western continent of night."[22] The rafting of goods ashore begins the new. The establishment of a domicile and an economy continues but does not complete the phase. The painstaking building of a boat, and Crusoe's efforts to move ever onward from the Island of Despair represent for Thoreau the never-ending process. Crusoe is ship-wrecked *into* life.

Thoreau's idea that "mankind's progress from east to west" to a hopefully better life has been hastily condemned as chauvinism.[23] Such a reading, however, is too confined, if not merely contentious. He said: Commercialism, with its crutch, politics, "has its place merely." He was interested philosophically in the sidereal movement of society and interestingly enough anticipates the view of the modern existential philosopher José Ortega in *Living History*. It is quite true that Thoreau allows for the obvious material promise of the Western World. The "children of exhausted Europe exposed on her uninhabited and savage shores," suckled like Romulus and Remus and "having derived new life and vigor from her breast, have founded a new Rome in the West." In *Walking* he takes the "encouraging testimonies" of Arnold Guyot, the younger Michaux, Sir Francis Head, and Linnaeus in stride. He copied out from Guyot, "The New World is the humid side of our planet, the oceanic, vegetative world, the passive element awaiting the excitement of a livelier impulse from without," but he himself observed that "some of the sand of the Old World" is needed to be carted onto the "as yet unassimilated meadows."[24]

His is obviously an ideal version of the American dream, of which he reminds us over and over. The whole westward movement is "symbolic of the path we love to travel in the interior and ideal world." The signs of material betterment "are symbolic of the height to which the philosophy and poetry and religion of [Americans] may one day soar." This gives the necessary intensity to Thoreau's italics in the remark, "I felt that *this was the heroic age itself.*" Yet the concept was larger than America alone, "for the world is America, a New World." A mere "*culture*" cannot express it. And so he decides, "Mythology comes nearer to it than anything," with the West "preparing to add its fables to those of the East."[25]

In this context, Robinson Crusoe was for him especially American, the shattered European standing on a new shore with a revived dream of infinite possibility. He belonged with countless others in Thoreau's poem, "Our Country," where Americans are "the far-traveled race," the "so long gathering congress of the world!" With them "earth's inhabitants" are invited to "rear their lives to an unheard-of height"

And meet the expectation of the land;
To give at length the restless race of man
A pause in the long westering caravan.[26]

To meet the expectaton of the land! The real westward migrant may arrive somewhere and establish a permanent home. Spiritual westering, however, is a series of Walden-like pauses (harbors, shores) where men may refit themselves like ships in order to go on. Thoreau nowhere says, like the assured Emerson in *The Young American*, that such *will* happen, nor that America *is* the "home of man." He takes a longer view and hammers away at the restlessness of man, who with courage, tools, skills, and principle *may* seize the day and *can* do better than he has ever done. He may even learn to vibrate in response to the music of the universe. There are always more lives yet to live. The ship, the wreck, the raft, and the shore are symbols of action, and Now is the time for every man's Robinsoniad.

Three symbolic figures stand on Thoreau's symbolic shore: Thoreau himself (every sensitive man), the intensely American Cape Cod colossus, and Robinson Crusoe. The Crusoe experience modifies that of the Cape Cod man standing on the durable American shore presumably facing east. Thoreau's Robinson Crusoe stood on the American shore facing an ever-new West with the whole inner and outer world before him. He is the Cape man who has turned about and gone to work. Conventional death symbols in the idea of the West are not excluded; but that great "prophet" and mariner, Robinson Crusoe, presented in a single figure what the wood-chopper, sailor, or explorer also stood for. He belonged in the "mythology of America" (both Americas, that is) which Thoreau took to be mainly concerned with the spirit and potential of Man Renewable who might yet sit "in the earth as on a raft, listening to music that was not of the earth, but which ruled and arranged it. . . the harp articulate." This is where and what "man *should be*."

The Harvest of Thought

The world's a ship on its passage out.

Melville, subtitle of *White Jacket*

The ideal course of a thinking man is a voyage and a return to harbor—a round trip symbolizing his life.

"Autumnal Tints"

The autumn, then, is indeed a spring. All the year is a spring.

Journal

VIII

The Harvest of Thought

IN ADDITION TO ROBINSON CRUSOE, there was yet another man who came to fill Thoreau's thoughts at odd moments, especially when he made his periodic voyages up the Assabet River—Autumnal Man. However differently each figure worked on Thoreau's imagination, the focus of both inevitably came to rest on the rich associations of voyaging with the vitality of man's inner life. And both were finally inseparable, as we shall see, from the life-sustaining images of the maritime world that had excited Thoreau as a young man.

On October 22, 1853, Thoreau wrote in his *Journal*, "I cannot easily dismiss the subject of the fallen leaves." A few days before this he had been walking in woods that were alive, glowing, and audible with leaves dancing to their death. He had also been up the Assabet River, where he had been much impressed with masses of dry rustling curled-up leaves floating on the water. They reminded him of fleets of ships, enlarging for him a subject that he had been brooding over. The entry of October 22 expands into a description of these curious little craft and becomes the first and longest of several annual entries regarding such leaf-boats. Later he was to use the material from these in the "Fallen Leaves" section of "Autumnal Tints," rearranging details and adding more. In so doing he heightened the force and extended the meaning of "Autumnal Tints," his last completed and fully edited literary undertaking. His vehicle for accomplishing this was a nautical figure as subtle and compelling as any that preceded it.

Amidst all the picturesque color displayed in "Autumnal Tints" Thoreau is searching for the meaning of the autumn scene, unsung, as he says in the introduction, by any poet before him. His well-known comment about William Gilpin (whose famous works on the picturesque in nature he was commenting on early in 1854) is some indication of his concern. Gilpin, though an English divine, lacked moral sentiment, he complained, and was "conversant only with *visible forms*." "This is to give us the play of Hamlet with Hamlet left out."[1] In accord with this, Thoreau's "Fallen Leaves" becomes a long meditation on the significance of the great phenomenon of fall, including near the end of the cryptic remarks about the leaves, "They teach us how to die."[2] It has been easy to assume that Thoreau meant to express by this a wish for a beautiful human death, as graceful and enriching as that of the leaves. This is true to a certain extent. The autumnal tone was undoubtedly deepened, as has been averred, by signs of his own fatal sickness after 1855 and the sickness and peaceful death of his father in 1859. Nevertheless, Sherman Paul's reading made over twenty years ago[3] is still pertinent: "Autumnal Tints" is more vital than mortuary, more about living than dying, more about ripeness and ideas of harvest, than decay, however rich the mold. In this chapter I wish to reaffirm and extend Paul's reading of the essay (particularly of "Fallen Leaves") by calling attention to some hitherto unobserved conditions of mind lying back of the "visible forms" of the leaf-boat scenes. In this view the leaf-boats "teach us" to live so productively that we leave harvests of thought behind us when we die. Considered more narrowly, it means that Thoreau is presenting through the leaf-boats a metaphor for the ideal life of the philosopher-poet, the ideal which he held for himself, for, as he confided on March 7, 1859, human fruitage "is simply the higest use to which it can be put."[4]

Thoreau states his position over and over. The *Journal* in the decade of the 1850's is punctuated each autumn at harvest time with entries on the relation of color, ripeness, and thought. On September 2, 1851, he was thinking of his own crop, "the crop of crops, ripe thoughts, which glow and rustle and fill the air with fragrance for centuries."[5] Each autumn leaf displays the color of its "ripeness,"[6] he wrote two years later when he was first pondering the idea of compiling a book of painted leaves (November 22, 1853). In the fall of 1858 (a few months before he presented "Autumnal Tints" as a lecture) he returned to the idea of the autumnal mind: "Has not the mind, too, its harvest? Do not some scarlet leaves of thought come scatteringly down. . .?"[7] These variations on the theme of autumn obviously constitute the philosophical base of "Autumnal Tints." An almost monotonous repetition of the idea of ripeness runs through the introductory paragraphs. At the close of his chapter on the elm, which immediately precedes the meditation of fallen leaves, Thoreau pictures himself observing a marketman driving into Concord "with *his* crop," and Thoreau is "tempted to go thither, as to a husking of thoughts, now dry and ripe."[8] The fact that he rejects the idea as futile weakens in no way his concept of his own thoughts as his autumn crop. In "Fallen Leaves," comments on ripeness, crop, and color are repeated and are brilliantly made emblematic in the navigating leaf-boats. And finally "Autumnal Tints" closes with a comprehensive celebration of color, its picturesque importance in the landscape, and its rich contribution to the inner life of man. The general direction of Thoreau's poetic purpose in introducing the unusual leaf-boat scene seems clear.

For eight successive years (1853-1860), Thoreau paddled "up Assabet" in mid-October to see the leaves. Their fading colors, their movements on the water, and their crowding suggested from the very first a harbor scene, which he characteristically took care to present as more than picture. Annually his notes repeat his first impressions. The leaves rustle pleasantly. They seem to have been painted. They are light, tight, dry boats, dense cities of boats, like fleets in world ports. Repeated emphasis on color is intensified in 1858, prompted by a contrasting show of "painted ducks." They "often come and float among the painted leaves."[9] Color stands for all ripeness and success, the flower that precedes the fruit. The last entry (1860) simply records, "Wood ducks are about now, amid the painted leaves."[10]

In "Autumnal Tints" this vignette of masses of leaf-boats is expanded but is arranged in two separate scenes which at first seem needlessly repetitious, but which present fresh metaphorical emphasis through difference and contrast. The force of such contrast we feel through further knowledge of Thoreau's habitual language and his attitude toward leaf mold, winter, whaling, sounds in nature, and his regard for the life of the mind. All in all, Thoreau focuses on autumnal man himself and declares with Edgar of *King Lear* that ripeness is all. The passage in "Autumnal Tints" goes in the main as follows:

> When I go to the river the day after the principal fall of leaves, the sixteenth, I find my boat all covered... with the leaves of the golden willow...and I set sail with a cargo of them rustling under my feet.... When I turn into the mouth of the Assabet...large fleets of leaves are floating on its surface, as it were getting out to sea, with room to tack; but next the shore a little farther up, they are thicker than foam...still perfectly light and dry, with fibre unrelaxed; and at a rocky bend where they are met and stopped by the morning wind, they sometimes form a broad and dense crescent quite across the river. When I turn my prow that way, and the wave which it makes strikes them, list what a pleasant rustling...! Often it is their undulation only which reveals the water beneath them.... Or even in mid-channel...I hear them blown with a rustling sound....
>
> Perchance, in the afternoon of such a day, when the water is perfectly calm and full of reflections, I paddle gently down the main stream, and, turning up the Assabet, reach a quiet cove, where I unexpectedly find myself surrounded by myriads of leaves, like fellow voyagers, which seem to have the same purpose, or want of purpose, with myself. See this great fleet of scattered leaf-boats...each one curled up on every side by the sun's skill, each nerve a stiff spruce-knee, like boats of hide, and of all patterns,—

> Charon's boat probably among the rest,—and some lofty prows and poops, like the stately vessels of the ancients, scarcely moving in the sluggish current,—like the great fleets , the great Chinese cities of boats, with which you mingle on entering some great mart, some New York or Canton, which we are all steadily approaching together. How gently each has been deposited on the water! No violence has been used toward them yet, though, perchance palpitating hearts were present at the launching. And painted ducks, too, the splendid wood duck among the rest, often come to sail and float amid the painted leaves,—barks of a nobler model still![11]

Thoreau has here created fanciful harbor scenes so extensive and so mixed as to suggest universal human experience, a mass voyaging ending in well-known ports. The casual but uncertain mention of Charon's boat accepts the possibility that some vessels (not all) are already approaching the ultimate experience, death. But these harbors are unmistakably lively, busy places, the business of which is to send out ships and later to receive them back with all their various cargoes.

The scene is obviously double but with a designated difference between the two parts, a doubling not found among the entries in the *Journal*. In the first paragraph Thoreau is up the Assabet River in the morning; in the second he is up in the afternoon. In the morning he at once observes that the leaf-boats are getting *out* to sea with plenty of sailing room and much rustling sound; in the afternoon they are crowding quietly *into* port. As fellow voyager, Thoreau connects his own business with that of the leaves, heightened by mention of his own "cargo" of golden willow leaves. He too has been out on some sort of voyage and is getting on. The two concentrated scenes have been made to fit a pattern of human experience as symbolized by the act of sailing out to sea and the act of getting in to harbor, a prime example of the poetic process as described in his *Journal* for November 4, 1852: "My thought is part of the meaning of the world, and hence I use a part of the world as a symbol to express my thought."[12]

Just what did phrases like "bound out," "getting out," and "getting in" mean to Thoreau? With no need in his day to explain his language, he repeatedly speaks of himself in his *Journal* in the decade of the 1850's as "bound out" when he is engaged in winter's hard intellectual work. He is "getting in" when warm weather lures him from his study into the woods and fields and onto the Concord waterways. The two phrases thus represent two supplementary, mutually invigorating phases of his experience. They make the cycle of the year, of any great enterprise, of man's life itself. They derive basically from the calendar of whaling ships and others bound for the South Seas—out in fall or winter (Melville's famous *Pequod* sailed on December 25th), in during the spring of some later year. This was general knowledge, but it had come to Thoreau's attention rather vividly in December of 1854 when he was on his way to visit Daniel Ricketson in the suburbs of New Bedford, where instead of going directly to his host's house he went to the New Bedford docks. Here he found everything very quiet. "Saw casks of oil [whale oil]. . . . Town not lively; whalers abroad at this season,"[13] he wrote in his *Journal.*

His mind also held a store of vivid memories of actual ships he had seen in American waters. Provincetown, as we have seen, had provided him with lingering impressions of fleets of mackerel schooners which repeatedly had already served well for images to describe butterflies and ice crystals.[14] In the crowded harbors of Boston and New York, however, he had often noted with more than picturesque or Romantic interest the departure and arrival of unnumbered vessels. From Long Wharf he had gazed at them "successively unfurling their sails and getting to sea."[15] He also had seen flotillas of up to a hundred vessels "lying in the stream" in New York Harbor "ready to go to sea" when tide and wind were right.[16] He noted their drifting maneuvers when they first broke away from their crowded anchorage and then moved in a long procession from New York to Sandy Hook and out to all the ports of the world, as he reported from Staten Island in 1843. "I study the aspect of commerce at its Narrows here, where it passes in review before me,"[17] he wrote to Emerson on August 7. His feelings were mixed about such scenes in those days, but the vividness of the pictures remained indelible. The actions, he recognized, were global.

His memories of actual fleets of ships combined with a knowledge of the whaling calendar thus provide one important clue to the doubling of the Assabet leaf-boat scene. The significance of winter versus spring-summer activity, which—as we noted earlier in Chapter VI—took on a special personal meaning for Thoreau, provides another. His identification of winter as a rugged but profitable period of productive labor, the voayage symbolism of "bound out" and "getting in," and a long concern with the beauty and symbolism of leaves all come together in the long-pondered "Autumnal Tints." Remarks in *A Week* and a glancing remark in *Walden* anticipate it, and the *Journal* for years recorded regular seasonal notes. Though Thoreau confessed he had not got very far with a projected "book of leaves," the care he spent on "Autumnal Tints" warns that we might spend equal care in getting at its oily nut (or barrel) of meaning.

The very absence of autumn pageantry in *Walden* is understandable if we accept the possibility that Thoreau was holding this subject back for later, extensive treatment. Whereas he celebrated leaf-forms on the thawing railroad embankment in *Walden* and wrote eloquently on the leaf as evidence and symbol of all creation and all growth ("The Maker of this earth but patented a leaf,")[18] the great New England display of autumn color is surprisingly not there. In "Housewarming" he does observe that three small maples had started to turn. "Ah many a tale their color told! And gradually from week to week the character of each tree came out, and it admired itself reflected in the smooth mirror of the lake. Each morning the manager of this gallery substituted some new picture...."[19] That is all—an abstract statement about a picture. What tale it told was not to come until "Autumnal Tints."

Furthermore, "Autumnal Tints" seems to have been built around "Fallen Leaves." Thoreau divides the whole work into seven sections: "The Purple Grasses," "The Red Maple," "The Elm," "Fallen Leaves," "The Sugar Maple," "The Scarlet Oak," and (untitled) The Forest as a Garden. The key position of "Fallen Leaves," the pivotal center of the whole, is apparent. Against the extended catalogue of trees ablaze with color Thoreau projects his meditation on leaf mold, life and death, and universal ripeness. Within this middle, furthermore, there is a concentric middle, not just leaves on the forest floor nor on the streets of the town, but floating leaf-boats of "various pure and delicate tints."[20] There in the precise center of an essay otherwise bright with red and yellow colors of field and forest rests the russet nautical scene, colorful still, audible, and surcharged with action and life, integral to the whole instructive panorama.

Whereas the forest leaves gracefully skip and dance and rustle to their graves, annually enriching the life-sustaining soul, the faded curled-up leaf-boats are still at work sailing out and coming home. As Thoreau recalled them from his Assabet River excursions, those strong impressions that he could not get out of his mind back in 1853 were: 1) visible mass movements of tiny water craft, 2) much rustling sound,[21] 3) unseen undulations and implied actions, and 4) color with its symbolism of ripeness and fruitage in both nature and man. As finally composed for "Autumnal Tints," the little scenes show that nautical aspects, with their private meanings, have been intensified and expanded. To balance the quiet harbor scene of many craft *entering* a great port, he has revised and rearranged his material in order to create a preliminary scene consisting of leaf-boats *bound out*. Appropriate to this wholly nautical scene he has temporarily dropped his favorite figure of a red-coated warrior (symbolizing courage and virtue) and has displaced it with that of the sailor. On October 31 of that most colorful year of all, 1858, he noted in his *Journal*, "Each tree (in October) runs up its flag and we know [what] colors it sails under. The sailor sails, and the soldier marches, under a color which will report his virtues farthest, and the ship's 'private signals' must be such as can be distinguished at the greatest distance."[23] Thoreau, merging himself with the incoming voyagers, was presumably still sailing under the yellow signal of the morning's voyage out. And the whole day's voyagings ended with the particular observance of the spectacular irridescent-bronze and white-striped *living* wood ducks. The noblest barks of them all, they have been given the honor of climax; and they signal to the viewer through their brilliant coloring the ultimate universal theme, ripeness.

Of the general autumnal scene, Thoreau says that living and dying take place all the time, suppplementing one another. Leaves gracefully die, but their trees, well-nourished, live on. In the leaf-boat scenes, however, Thoreau tips the balance away from mere gracefulness in dying, toward life and its yield. He points to an enrichment beyond leaf or human mold. Death, recognized as universally fruitful, is made more specific. It is the final delivery point of the product of man's long labor—his rustling thoughts.

More narrowly, the Assabet diptych poetically reflects the fragile cyclic flow of living that sustains and justifies the thinking man. As leaves produce leaf mold, so thinking man produces hardearned "winter-strained" thought. "In October man is ripe even to his stalk and leaves," Thoreau set down (November 14, 1853) concerning that first Assabet adventure. "He is pervaded by his genius, when all the forest is universal harvest." The two harvests unite into one. The water-borne leaves "taught" him all over again how to live, by symbolizing the going out for winter's mental work and coming in with the products of that work. Thoreau's own cargo, therefore, must be *his* thoughts—his literary works.

Sherman Paul points particularly to the last essays as "the ripened fruit of the artist" wherein "natural things had become the transparent images of his thought."[23] The poetic leaf-boats are part of this very transparency. More obvious among Thoreau's literary harvests, however, must be his *Journal,* a depository which from the very beginning he associated with leaves. It began in autumn and it ended in autumn. It was a heap of the life-giving "Mould Our Deeds Leave,"[24] he wrote in his second entry, resolving at once that his whole life be autumnal, that is, pervaded by his genius. In his own context, thus, his major works, the *Week* and *Walden,* are also full of life-giving ripeness. And it is not inappropriate to note here that in the poetic expression of their substance, these works depend significantly on the ocean voyage as a strategic metaphor. The *Week* is thinly veiled as a deep-water voyage. *Walden* begins with a satirical picture of Thoreau as a shrewd South Sea trader and sweeps to its conclusion with his passionate exhortation to explore inner seas of thought. The leaf-boats in "Autumnal Tints" thus appear as Thoreau's last employment of a familiar metaphor for productive mental life. If to Melville "the world's a ship on its passage out," to Thoreau, man's mind is a ship that can and may come back with a full cargo.

If we speculate that Thoreau is here thinking of his own imminent death, we might reasonably assume that he felt he was approaching the teeming mart, a competent mariner who might dare to think he too all along had been dying well because he could deliver precious intellectual cargo, having "come home from far, from adventures, and perils, and new discoveries. . . with new experience and character," as recommended in *Walden.*[25] "Autumnal Tints" is, then, linked to all that went before, based as it is on ideas he had pondered for years, and expressing as it does some of his basic ideas and feelings about man's proper role in life. It refines and clarifies his conviction that man's basic responsibility is to observe his world, define what he considers his highest function, and do his best to express it—the Herculean task of thinking a thought about life and getting it well expressed.

ACKNOWLEDGEMENTS

I have received much stimulation and enlightenment from F.O. Matthiessen's classic *American Renaissance* (New York, 1941), Reginald Cook's *Passage to Walden* (Boston, 1949) and "This Side of Walden" in *The English Leaflet* for Dec., 1954 (Vol. LIII), R.W.B. Lewis's *The American Adam* (Chicago, 1955), James Lyndon Shanley's *The Making of Walden* (Chicago, 1957), Sherman Paul's *The Shores of America* (Chicago, 1965), John Aldrich Christie's *Thoreau as World Traveller* (New York, 1965), and Charles R. Anderson's *The Magic Circle of Walden* (New York, 1968). Leo Marx's *The Machine in the Garden* (New York, 1964) lends weight to my argument for a need to understand Thoreau's middle position.

My work has run parallel to that of Paul and Christie at times, acknowledgement of which is made in the proper places. Leo Stoller's *After Walden* (Stanford, 1957) presented a challenge which I have accepted and countered. And I have used the stores of fact and information in Walter Harding's many works.

I am indebted otherwise to many persons and institutions, especially Mr. M. Runge of the University of Virginia Library, Mrs. Marcia Moss and the Concord Free Library, the Boston Public Library, The Lockwood Memorial Library of the State University of New York at Buffalo, the Bowdoin College Library, Mr. Maurice G. Lauson and the New Bedford *Standard-Times,* and the State University of New York for a Faculty Summer Research Grant. A paper by Mary Alice Budge was the starting point for Chapter VII.

The following journals have generously provided space for early drafts of and excerpts from my manuscript when in process: *American Literature* (XXXIV, No. 4, Jan., 1963), *Canadian Association for American Studies Bulletin* (III, No. 2, Winter, 1968), *The New England Quarterly* (XXXIX, No. 1, March, 1966), *The Concord Saunterer* (VIII, No. 1, March, 1973), *Thoreau Journal Quarterly* (V, No. 2, April, 1973), and *Emerson Society Quarterly* (XXII, 2nd quarter, 1976).

Professor Laurence Michel was kind enough to give a first draft of the manuscript a firm critical reading, and Mrs. Hilda Ludwig combined patience with skill beyond the call of a secretary.

W.H.B.

WORKS FREQUENTLY REFERRED TO

Cue	*Title*
Wr	*The Writings of Henry David Thoreau,* Walden Edition (Boston, 1906) in 20 volumes, of which the last 14 are the separately numbered and paged *Journal.*
J	*The Journal of Henry D. Thoreau,* ed. Bradford Torrey and Francis H. Allen, as it appears in the Walden Edition (above) and separately published in two large volumes by Dover Publications (N.Y., 1962).
Corr.	*The Correspondence of Henry David Thoreau,* ed. Walter Harding and Carl Bode (N.Y., 1958).
Poems	*Collected Poems of Henry Thoreau,* ed. Carl Bode, enlarged edition (Baltimore, 1965).
Am. Ren.	F.O. Matthiessen, *American Renaissance* (N.Y., 1941).
Miller	Perry Miller, *Consciousness in Concord* (Boston, 1958). an editing of an early and long lost volume of Thoreau's *Journal.* The long introduction is famous for its controversial analysis of Thoreau's character.
R C	*Robinson Crusoe,* ed. Charles Whibley, 3 vols. (London, 1925). These are reprints of original editions, as follows: Vol. I, 3rd ed.; Vol. II, 2nd ed.; Vol. III, 1st ed.

NOTES

Referential and Gratuitous

Chapter I

1. J. Lyndon Shanley, *Walden* (Princeton University Press, 1971), p. 359.
2. Harrison Hayford, "Hawthorne, Melville, and the Sea," *New England Quarterly*, Vol. XIX, No. 4 (Dec., 1946), p. 447.
3. J, VIII, 99.
4. *New England and the South Seas* (Harvard University Press, 1965), 186–187.
5. J, II, 344.
6. "The Dialectical Imagination," *New York Times Book Review*, Oct. 28, 1973, p. 32.

Chapter II

1. J, II, 178. References to Thoreau's writings are to the Walden Edition of 1906, cue "Wr". As the volumes of the *Journal* (ed. Torrey and Allen) are separately paged and numbered, reference is directly to it, cue "J".
2. J, III, 416–417.
3. J, XII, 249; III, 418; XI, 242.
4. Lawrence E. Richardson, *Concord River* (Barre, Mass., 1964) p. 30; Wr, I, 32.
5. J, VII, 461.
6. J, V, 211–212.
7. J, XII, 253.
8. J, V, 451; XIII, 419–421; *Freeman*, May 9, 1835; J, III, 440.
9. Wr, I, 326–327; IV, 282–283; J, II, 225; VII, 512.
10. Wr, IV, 182; J, XI, 238; Wr, I, 257; F.B. Sanborn, *Henry D. Thoreau* (Boston, 1882), pp. 66–67.
11. J, III, 126–127.
12. J, VII, 69–70; VIII, 419; IX, 168–169.
13. Wr, II, 212.
14. J, VII, 185.
15. Walter Harding, *The Days of Henry Thoreau* (N.Y., 1965), p. 4.
16. J, V, 242–243; Harding, *The Days*, 4–5.
17. Besides "merchant" and "grocer" and aside from specialties like "iron monger," "sail maker," and "painter," other names for shops and shopkeepers were: "shop-keeper," "goods store," "West India store," "retailer," "importer," and "grocer." The *Boston Directory* for 1789 calls Thoreau's establishment a "store" and locates it at No. 45.
18. *Boston Looks Seaward. The Story of the Port, 1630-1940* (Boston, 1941), p. 70. In the W.P.A. *American Guide Series.*
19. *The Maritime History of Massachusetts* (Boston, 1961), p. 252.
20. Wr, IV, 268.

21. *Ibid.*, I, 224–225.
22. J, IV, 465–466; III, 439; IV, 465.
23. Townsend Scudder, *Concord, An American Town* (Boston, 1947), pp. 139, 104.
24. Thoreau charted (measured and sounded) not only Walden Pond but Concord River. This interacted with his intense interest in the 1850's in the work of and the reports issued by the U.S. Coast and Geodetic Survey, which Government Service was of incalculable use to shipping. His friend Eben J. Loomis in Washington kept him supplied with the Survey reports as well as the *U.S. Nautical Almanac.* Professor Leo Stoller has made the interesting remark, apropos of the spread of Thoreau's interest from sandbars across Walden coves to the same across harbor mouths, "Only a short distance separated the subsistence experiment at Walden from Boston with its docks and warehouses." *(After Walden* [Stanford, 1957], pp. 44-45.)

Chapter III

1. J, VI, 229; VIII, 422.
2. *Corr.*, 8–9.
3. J, XIII, 226–227.
4. J, IV, 225–226.
5. J, X, 145.
6. Wr, I, 227–228.
7. J, IV, 325.
8. J, IV, 328.
9. J, V, 404.
10. J, VI, 246–248; VIII, 317.
11. J, XII, 98.
12. *Corr.*, 484; Wr, I, 253.
13. *The American Notebooks,* ed. Randall Stewart, 1932, 168.
14. J, II, 359–360; IV, 327.
15. Wr, I, 362.
16. J, IV, 325; VIII, 299.
17. J, III, 74–75.
18. J, III, 357.
19. J, II, 375.
20. John Aldrich Christie, *Thoreau as World Traveller* (New York, 1965), 121–122.
21. J, II, 406; III, 8–9.
22. Wr, V, 224.
23. J, XIV, 261.
24. J, XIV, 49.
25. Wr, II, 363.
26. *Am. Ren.,* 629.
27. James L. Shanley, *The Making of Walden* (Chicago, 1957), 173. "Sailor-like" drops out in the final version of *Walden.* For Thoreau's ambivalent attitude toward Therien, see Robert W. Bradford, "Thoreau and Therien," *American Literature,* XXIV (Jan., 1963), 499-506.

Chapter IV

1. The young Thoreau amused himself and his correspondents with linguistic foolery in a number of vocabularies: Indian, Nautical, Cowboy, Military, etc. For a thick mix of nautical and cowboy terms, see J, I, 188.
2. MUSIC (marching to music, the wind harp, the telegraph), WALKING (traveling, the traveler, sauntering), PHENOMENA OF LANDSCAPE (especially mountains and trees), FRESH WATER (lakes, ponds, small streams), AERIAL PHENOMENA (wind, fog, clouds), LIGHT (and darkness), GROWTH (and decay).
3. J, IV, 399.
4. J, X, 99.
5. J, IX, 18, 22–23.
6. Wr, IV, 259–260.
7. Wr, I, 358.
8. J, I, 353.
9. Miller, 212.
10. J, XIII, 385–386.
11. J, XII, 278.
12. J, VIII, 407.
13. J, VII, 169.
14. J, XIII, 140.
15. J, VII, 160–161.
16. J, XI, 224–225.
17. J, III, 105.
18. Wr, II, 334.
19. *Am. Ren.,* 152.
20. *Cape Cod,* Wr. IV, 29.
21. J, IV, 139.
22. Thoreau rejected the "Oh, how she schoons!" theory of the origin of the term, from the supposed launching of the first schooner at Gloucester, and preferred to think it came from an Indian word.
23. J, VII, 452.
24. J, III, 162; IV, 345; XIV, 29.
25. J, V, 298–299.
26. *Coll. Poems,* rev. ed., 292–294; J, III, 201.
27. See Chapter VIII for a fuller discussion of "Autumnal Tints."
28. XI, 314.

Chapter V

1. J, VI, 294–295.
2. "Paradise (to be) Regained," Wr, IV, 289.
3. J, III, 484; XI, 384.
4. J, IX, 349.
5. Wr, I, 229, 78; J, I, 54.
6. J, IV, 289; II, 486-487; V, 216-217; *Poems,* 150. He had heard talk of the sea serpent at Plymouth.

7. J, XII, 51; X, 317, 438.
8. J, III, 142–144; XI, 450–451.
9. J, XI, 305–306.
10. J, X, 169; XI, 242.
11. Wr, I, 5; J, X, 498; Cf. Allen and the *Journal, passim.*
12. Arch and amusing is Thoreau's complaint to Emerson that the lines in Emerson's Ode to Beauty "slope too quickly to the rhyme," and that the ends seem chopped off. Thoreau nevertheless adds that he loves Emerson's poetry as he does "little else that is near and recent, especially when you get fairly round the end of the line, and are not thrown back on the rocks." (*Corr.,* 145–146). That was one headland at least that got rounded.

    Recovering from a violent nausea caused by eating a whole clam at Wellfleet on the Cape, Thoreau whimsically remarked to his merry old host, "I believe I have weathered the clam cape."

    The seashore as both a point of arrival and a point of departure is to be seen in Thoreau's fascination with the most famous shipwreck in fiction, that of Robinson Crusoe. The symbolism of this is taken up in Chapter VII, "Homeric Indiaman."
13. Pp. 113, 168.
14. Wr, IV, 11–12.
15. J, I, 217–218.
16. Wr, IV, 115, 12.
17. *Poems* (1965), 360.
18. Miller, 179.
19. J, I, 239, 163, 28, 40; Wr, V, 242.
20. Wr, I, 255. These four stanzas were reprinted in Thoreau's lifetime in *Thallatta: A Book for the Seaside* (Boston, 1853), p. 196. A Boston newspaper described the collection of poems as "a happy thought of Mr. [Samuel] Longfellow and Mr. [T.W.S.] Higgenson." It suggests a kind of public image of Thoreau as the (probably uncomfortable) poet of the fashionable seaside resorts he publicly chastised.
21. Miller, 213.
22. Wr, I, 74; J, II, 251.
23. J, XII, 233–236.
24. *Poems,* 201–202.
25. Wr, IV, 186–189, 122–123, 127.
26. Wr, IV, 218.
27. J, XIV, 117.
28. John McAleer is tentative on Thoreau's remark and resolves the difficulty by asserting that Thoreau's negatives were "the preface to affirmatives." ("Thoreau's Epic Cape Cod,' " *Thought,* Fordham University Quarterly, XLIII, No. 169 [1968] p. 246.)
29. Wr, IV, 71. Edward Stephenson discusses this particular point in "Longfellow Revisited," *Thoreau Society Bulletin,* No. 118 (1972), pp. 4-5.
30. *Corr.,* 558.
31. J, I, 26–28.

Chapter VI

1. Wr, V, 143.
2. *The Shores of America* (1958), 201. Paul's summary conclusion is that Thoreau's whole life was an exploration.
3. Wr, I, 253.
4. J, XI, 4–5, I, 58–59; Wr, I, 105–106.
5. The seeming imbalance among the names that Thoreau lumps together would not seem odd to Boston merchants and sea captains, who controlled the Northwest fur trade. Unknown today, Ledyard was an electrifying figure. He not only sailed on Captain Cook's last voyage and published the account of it that Americans read, but he was principally responsible for making known the possibilities of the fur trade that was to center in Nootka Sound, B.C. and would open up the Oregon country. Thomas Jefferson in Paris was much taken with this "young man of genius, some science and of fearless courage and enterprise," who was planning an expedition to the West Coast with John Paul Jones. Jefferson later wrote a book about him. His trek across Siberia by dog sled was spectacular, and Melville called him, "Ledyard the great New England traveler."
6. J, XIV, 260, 261, 262.
7. J, I, 363.
8. See James L. Shanley, *The Making of Walden* (Chicago, 1957).
9. Attention might be called to the fact that the entry in Thoreau's *Journal* (III, 214–215) that was the immediate source of the "deck of the world" passage contained several parallel metaphors clustered around the idea of transportation and theater tickets. In *Walden* Thoreau dropped the others in favor of the nautical—a ship's passenger who has paid his way. The *Journal passage* includes the following:

> Perhaps if I lived there [Walden Pond] much longer, I might live there forever. One would think twice before he accepted heaven on such terms. A ticket to Heaven must include tickets to Limbo, Purgatory, and Hell. Your ticket to the boxes admits you to the pit also. And if you take a cabin passage, you can smoke, at least forward of the engine,—and you have the liberty of the whole boat. But no, I do not wish for a ticket to the boxes, nor to take a cabin passage. I will rather go before the mast and on the deck of the world. I have no desire to go "abaft the engine."

   Playful comments by Melville in *Moby Dick* and serious ones by Dana in *Two Years Before the Mast* reflect common knowledge of, and a new concern for, the distinction between the soft life of the fare-paying passenger and the hard life of the working sailor. Indeed, Dana wrote his book in order to depict for the first time just what life was like in the forecastle of an American merchantman. Cooper tardily (1849) makes a similar claim for his novel *The Pilot,* published first in 1823.
10. Wr, II, 101–102.
11. Wr, II, 156, 297, 159.

12. Wr, II, 321–322.
13. Wr, IX, 70.
14. Wr, IX, 83.
15. Wr, IX, 232.
16. Wr, IX, 207.
17. Wr, IX, 233.
18. Wr, XII, 84–85.
19. Wr, XII, 87.
20. Wr, XVIII, 52.
21. Wr, XVIII, 176–177.
22. J, I, 77; *Corr.,* 158–159. The italics are Thoreau's.
23. J, XII, 159–160, 224–225.
24. J, III, 358. See also 332–333.
25. J, III, 80–82.
26. The mention of dead men's buttons derives from Thoreau's search along the beach at Fire Island for the bodies of Margaret Fuller and her husband the Marquis of Ossoli, a year before. He wrote to Harrison Blake (Aug. 9, 1850):

    > This petty stream which from time to time swells and carries away the mills and bridges of our habitual life, and that mightier stream or ocean on which we securely float,—what makes the difference between them? I have in my pocket a button which I ripped off the coat of the Marquis of Ossoli, on the seashore, the other day. Held up, it intercepts the light,—an actual button,—and yet all the life it is connected with is less substantial to me, and interests me less, than my faintest dream.

    It is of interest in connection with the persistence of Thoreau's nautical imagery that three years later (May 23, 1854), in his most anguished cry over lost powers, he is in the final metaphor a wrecked seaman. For an image of inert failure and loss, the skuttle of dirt of the 1851 dream is replaced with a dead pickerel floating, "the vignette of the year." For the flute, image of articulate power, he substitutes other musical instruments, mainly the wind harp, which being identified with himself lies foundered on the seashore no longer responsive to the winds.
27. Paul, "The Wise Silence," *New England Quarterly,* XXII (Dec., 1949), 526–527; J, V, 17.
28. Wr, IV, 320, 322–323, 349, 350.
39. Wr, IV, 306–310.
30. Professor Carl Bode's Textual Notes in the Enlarged Edition (Baltimore, 1965) of the *Poems* are a mine of useful information.
31. "An Evaluation of Thoreau's Poetry," *American Literature,* XVI (May, 1944), reprinted by Sherman Paul, *Thoreau* (1962), 139.
32. *Poems,*210. Other poems noticeably nautical are:

    General
    "The Shrike" (is a ship)
    "Man's Little Acts Are Grand" (ships)
    "The Vessel of Love, The Vessel of State" (ballasted with hate)
    "Though All the Fates..." (New England's worm in the hull)

Personal

"The Old Marlborough Road" (man a ship, fancy the sail)
"I Am Bound for a Distant Shore" (the navigator)
"I Sailed Up a River" (river as ocean)
"The Atlantides" (love, a mid-Atlantic mystery)
"My Love Must Be As Free" (poet is mariner)
"All Things Are Current Found" (intense feeling for the shore)
"The Friend" (a beacon on the shore)
"My Years Are Like A Stroll Upon the Beach (the vitalizing shore)
"Life" (is a ship)
"In Times of Yore" (if three men in a bowl, why not I in a bread-trough of a boat?)

Chapter VII

1. Reginald L. Cook, "This Side of Walden" in *The English Leaflet* for Dec., 1954, Vol. LIII, p. 2.
2. References to *Robinson Crusoe* are to the Whibley edition, 3 vols. (London, 1925). Cue: R C.
3. It is well to bear in mind that Thoreau always spoke of Robinson Crusoe as a real, historical person. He never mentions Defoe nor reveals any awareness that Defoe's tale was a piece of fiction.
4. The only person, I suspect, who has taken the trouble to look up Wolff's *Narrative* (1845) is John Aldrich Christie, who reports that Wolff took along to Bokhara more translations of *Robinson Crusoe* than Bibles, and that Defoe's story was read in the market places and was admired and believed.
5. Wr, I, 59–61; Matthiessen, *Am. Ren.*, 646–647.
6. Alexander Selkirk, a really marooned man, lived four years and four months alone on the island of Juan Fernandez in the Pacific off the coast of Chile. Crusoe's Island of Despair was in the Atlantic off the mouth of the Orinoco River, where Crusoe spent slightly over twenty-eight years. Yet Thoreau refers to "Robinson Crusoe in the Pacific" (J, I, 129) and to the footprint that surprised Robinson Crusoe "on the shore of Juan Fernandez." (J, II, 328)
7. Some idea of this is gained from juxtaposing moments and phrases from *Crusoe.* The italics are mine.

From R.C.:

I traveled for discovery up to the top of a hill. I saw I was in an island *environed* every way *with the sea.* (I, 60)

I began to make a more particular *survey* of the island itself. (I, 113)

I was *king and lord* of *all this country.* (I, 116)

I was *lord* of the *whole manor.* (I, 149)

I might call myself *king* or *emperor* over the *whole country.* (I, 150)

There were *no rivals...none to dispute sovereignty.* (I, 150)

to make a *tour round the island* (I, 159)

viewing the sea from that hill (I, 161)

my *majesty prince* and *lord of the whole island* (I, 173)

I had the lives of all *my subjects* at my *absolute command* ... Poll, my dog ... two cats ... my cattle, that is to say, my goats (I, 173)

Stanza No. 1 from Cowper's "Verses Suppposed to be Written by Alexander Selkirk":

I am *monarch* of all I *survey,*
My *right* there is *none to dispute;*
From the center *around to the sea,*
I am *lord of* the *fowl* and the *brute.*

It is Cowper, therefore, who merged the real and fictional figures for all who followed him, including Thoreau.

8. Wr, I, 257–258. Italics are mine.
9. Wr, I, 307–308; J, IX, 351–352.
10. R C, I, 86; Wr, II, 50, 52.
11. Wr, II, 100–101; R C, I, 112, 150.
12. We do not know whether Thoreau read these last volumes, wherein the ageing Crusoe, after engaging in many trading adventures on the China Coast, comes back home along the Siberian caravan routes and finally sits down to compose his *Serious Reflections,* beginning: "I must have made very little of my solitary and wandering years, if...I had nothing to say, and had made no observations that might be useful...." He has much to say on the subject of solitude, the world vs. retirement, etc. (Compare Thoreau sending his *Walden* letter home from some distant land, to be of use possibly to some poor students.) In this part of *Robinson Crusoe* Defoe speaks through the voice of a Russian Count—from our point of view in time a strongly Thoreauvian voice:

> He found more felicity in the retirement he seem'd to be banish'd to than he ever knew at the Czar's court, that the height of human wisdom was to bring our tempers down to our circumstances, and to make a calm within, under the weight of the greatest storm without...the mind of man was perfectly capable of making a felicity for itself...that the air to breathe in, food to sustain life, clothes for warmth, and liberty for exercise...compleated...all that the world could do for us...virtue only makes a man truly wise, rich, and great. (R C, II, 315–316)

Yet Crusoe, though continuing his praise of solitude in the *Serious Reflections,* shifts his ground, insisting on man's capacity to be alone in the crowd, though "As for contentment in an island, if the scene was plac'd there for this very end, were not at all amiss." His point is the curiously modern one that "Everything revolves in our minds by innumerable circular motions, all centering in ourselves." (R C, III, 1–3)

13. R C, I, 210.
14. "Introduction," *Walden and Civil Disobedience,* 1960, xxvii.

15. Wr, II, 18, 39.
16. Wr, I, 280; J, IX, 298 and I, 129.
17. Wr, IV, 11–13.
18. *Corr.,* 286; J, XI, 276–277.
19. J, III, 99; I, 412.
20. Wr, V, 210.
21. *Clarel,* Part IV, "Bethlehem," xxi, ll. 167–169; Wr, V, 218; IV, 178. Matthiessen, *Am. Ren.,* 647.
22. J, VI, 53.
23. No critic has understood the "westering caravan" as clearly as Christie in the final chapter of *Thoreau as World Traveler,* 1965. Carl Bode seems to accept these enthusiasms as "Fourth-of-July nationalism." (*Poems,* 362).
24. J, II, 147–151.
25. J, III, 384.
26. *Poems,* 135; Wr, V, 224–236 *passim.*

Chapter VIII

1. Wr, XII, 59.
2. Wr, V, 278.
3. Paul, *The Shores of America,* 400–407. A sensitive Japanese view of "Autumnal Tints" by Prof. Koh Kasegawa contains the latest expression I have seen of the mistaken importance of a death theme. See "Color in Nature: A View of Autumnal Tints," *Thoreau Journal Quarterly,* International Issue, 7 (1975), 20–24. My reading of parts of "Autumnal Tints" is necessarily more confined and more detailed than those of Bernard Rosenthal and B. Bernard Cohen in *Emerson Society Quarterly* (No. 56, 1969). Rosenthal, who sees "Autumnal Tints" as Thoreau's final testament, pays attention to ironic wordplay and the theme of unity in autumn's variety. Cohen emphasizes light and perspective and briefly sees the harbor scene as a symbol of every man's voyage toward death.
4. Wr, XVIII, 24.
5. Wr, VIII, 442.
6. Wr, XI, 516.
7. Wr, XVII, 130.
8. Wr, V, 264.
9. Wr, XVII, 216.
10. Wr, XX, 108.
11. Wr, V, 266–268.
12. Wr, IV, 410.
13. Wr, XIII, 90.
14. Good examples of these may be seen in X, 226–227; VIII, 157.
15. Wr, XII, 250.
16. Wr, VI, 82.
17. Wr, VI, 70, 72.
18. Wr, II, 340.
19. Wr, II, 265.
20. Wr, V, 268.

21. Rustling sounds in nature haunted Thoreau. In *A Week on the Concord and Merrimack Rivers* and in many places in the Journal, such sounds stand for thoughts and universal energies lying back of the face of nature. Starting home on Friday, "listening to the sigh of the first autumnal wind," the two navigators found that their "thoughts, too, began to rustle" (Wr, I, 358). The autumnal aspect of *A Week on the Concord and Merrimack Rivers* has recently been emphasized by Carol Krob, who presents the river journey as a poetical exercise in preparation for intellectual harvest. See "Columbus of Concord: *A Week* as a Voyage of Discovery," *ESQ,* 21 (1975), 220–221.
22. Wr, XVII, 269.
23. Paul, *The Shores of America,* 403.
24. Wr, VII, 3.
25. Wr, II, 231.

Index